Adult Christianity

ADULT CHRISTIANITY

by

Hilda Graef

DEUS BOOKS
Paulist Press
(Paulist Fathers)
Glen Rock, N.J.

A Deus Books Edition of the Paulist Press, 1966, by special arrangement with Franciscan Herald Press, Chicago, Illinois.

Nihil Obstat: Rev. James J. O'Connor
                                    Censor Librorum

Imprimatur: Leo A. Pursley, D.D.
                    Bishop of Fort Wayne-South Bend

June 28, 1966

Cover Design: Claude Ponsot

Published by the Paulist Press
Editorial Office: 304 W. 58th St., N.Y., N.Y. 10019
Business Office: Glen Rock, New Jersey 07452

Manufactured in the
United States of America
by Our Sunday Visitor

Contents

A Sense of Wonder

Oᴜʀ modern Western world has become very sophisticated. The tremendous technological development of the last fifty years has brought about in most of us a state of mind that is no longer surprised at anything and believes implicitly that all things are possible — to the scientists. Whether it is a matter of space-travel or test tube babies, we take everything in our stride. We seem to have lost a very important sense: the sense of wonder.

This sense is, of course, still present in children, but even in them it ceases to function at a very early age. As they watch television almost from babyhood the marvels of science as well as the beauties of foreign countries become completely familiar to them, nothing holds a mystery for them any more, everything seems quite commonplace; for the old saying that familiarity breeds contempt is unfortunately very true. For this reason man's sense of wonder was much more active when the laws of nature were practically unknown and spirits were invented to account for the movements of the stars and were believed to inhabit forests and springs. Yet the universe as these primitive men imagined it was infinitely more intelligible than ours. And not only primitive man's universe. Even such sophisticated people as the ancient Greeks, indeed all men prior to the sixteenth century (except for some soon forgotten and ridiculed geniuses), believed in a neat little cosmos with the earth in its centre and sun, moon and stars circling round it. They also believed in a God who had made it. For though the universe as it appeared to them was so much smaller than we know it to be, it nevertheless held many marvels which struck man's imagination and led him to believe that it could not have come into being of its own account.

Today many of us no longer hold such a view. Together with our knowledge of an infinitely larger and more complex universe than our ancestors ever dreamt of, we have come to accept it as a fact that the world came into being by itself, whether it evolved from a hydrogen atom or in some other way. We pronounce the magic word 'evolution' and assume that this explains everything. But for something to evolve there must first exist something from which it evolves and, further, this 'something' must in itself already contain the possibility to evolve into the finished product. For we know from experience that an acorn cannot develop into a chicken nor a hen egg into an oak tree. The hydrogen atom from which the world is believed by many scientists to have evolved must have contained the potentialities to evolve into just this world that we know.

Now the scientists do not tell us how this atom first came into existence, nor how it came to contain all the possibilities of its further evolution. This is beyond their province to explain, and indeed the human mind is too small to be able to explain it, provided this hypothesis of the origin of the world—and it is no more than a hypothesis—should be true. But because it is so easily accepted, without its implications even being considered, men have largely lost their sense of wonder; they accept what they are told without further thought or questioning.

Nevertheless, without this sense of wonder the world loses a whole dimension, and a dimension which is necessary to the mind of man. For it is through the sense of wonder that we ask questions, and without asking questions we cannot even give scientific answers, let alone attempt to penetrate into the deeper causes of things. For the sense of wonder is a creative sense. Without it man would never have become civilized. One might even suggest that without the sense of wonder man would not be man. For every discovery, every invention is due in some measure to the sense of wonder. The animal does not wonder; it takes things as it finds them; true, its instinct tells it to build nests, to store food up for the winter; but it does not go further. Its activities are strictly limited to its basic needs.

Man, on the other hand, struck two stones together, wondering what would happen—and discovered fire. He wondered how he could communicate to others his thoughts—and invented language. He wondered how he could give permanence to his words—and invented various forms of script. When he had reached a stage at which his thoughts became more abstract he concerned himself with the reason of things and became a philosopher. He wondered how he and the world around him had come into being and found God.

For the strange thing is that there is an answer to the questioning wondering of man. His mind encounters his surroundings, his fellow-men, the earth and the whole universe. And in this encounter there is a response. For man can come to understand his surroundings, at least partially and progressively. He discovers mathematics, and he realizes that much of the world in which he lives can be explained by it. He makes instruments like telescopes, microscopes, Geiger counters—and both constellations and atoms yield up many of their secrets. This means that the phenomena he meets in the world are accessible to man's mind, which can investigate and very often also explain them. But could man's reason understand the world if it were altogether irrational? On the other hand, if the world is not irrational, but can be investigated by the human mind and made to yield up its secrets to its wondering questions, does this not mean that there must be some intelligence behind this world of phenomena?

To give an example of what I mean. We may give a heap

of letters cut from cardboard to a small child or an illiterate man to arrange. He will put them together quite arbitrarily, and the result will be meaningless. But give the same letters to a person who can read and write, and he will form them into words which others can understand. True, this is a very crude example, but it will serve our purpose. For it seems to me that unless the world were arranged by a mind, however different from our human minds, we simply could not make sense of it. If everything happened in a quite haphazard way we could not find laws in it; the world around us would be completely closed to our investigation. But as it quite obviously is open to this intellectual investigation, it seems that there must be intelligence behind it.

This does not mean that every happening in the world must be particularly arranged by this 'mind behind it'. For this view does not at all exclude the idea of evolution. But it does mean that the evolutionary process itself has been set in motion by a mind, that the wonder in man's mind which leads him to examine the world corresponds to a mind behind the world, challenging man to investigate its laws and to find answers to its riddles.

It is one of the great tragedies of modern times that science and religion have been at cross purposes for the last four centuries, and only recently men like the French Jesuit archaeologist Teilhard de Chardin have endeavoured to bridge the gap between the two. When Copernicus and Galileo first made their great discoveries in the sixteenth and seventeenth centuries they were rejected by most Christians, both Catholic and Protestant, because they seemed to contradict not only the teaching of the Bible about the creation of the world, but also the whole of Christian tradition, which had for fifteen hundred years been based on the firm belief that the earth was the immovable centre of the universe, around which moved sun, moon and stars. When Copernicus and Galileo announced that the truth was exactly the reverse, that the earth was moving round the sun, in common with other planets, the whole Christian world seemed to have been turned upside down. And when, after three centuries, Christians had finally adapted their ideas to a new picture of the universe, nineteenth century scientists had another blow in store for them: the theory of evolution, which many of them have not been able to accept even yet.

For until then Christians had believed that all species had been created separately by God; now Darwin taught that they had evolved from one common ancestor. Darwin's system has been modified by later scientists, but archaeological finds have proved beyond a doubt that even man himself has evolved slowly from more primitive forms, though when and how the decisive step from hominid to man was taken is still unknown. In his grandiose vision of the evolution of the 'Phenomenon of Man' Teilhard de Chardin suggests that when the time was ripe the 'explosion' of mind occurred in the hominid, and man as we know him emerged.

Teilhard was a sincere Christian, but of a mind sufficiently deep and broad to accommodate both his faith

12

and his scientific knowledge; he did not fear that the results of his research might upset his religion; rather, indeed, they strengthened it. For in him the sense of wonder was very profound; he himself tells how, even when he was still quite a small boy, he would get hold of a piece of iron and repeat again and again, with intense awe: 'God. Iron.' For him there was no unbridgeable gulf between God and matter, between religion and science. The wonder of the world, of matter, and the wonder of God were intimately linked with each other.

It is time to stress that to investigate the world of nature can be a profoundly religious activity; indeed, in one of the biblical books printed among the apocrypha in the Authorized and Revised Versions, the so-called Wisdom of Solomon, the investigation of nature is presented as one of the activities taught the author by God himself: 'For himself gave me an unerring knowledge of the things that are, to know the constitution of the world, and the operation of the elements; the beginning and end and middle of times, the alternations of the solstices and the changes of seasons, the circuits of years and the position of stars, the natures of living creatures and the ragings of wild beasts. . . . All things that are either secret or manifest I learned, for she that is the artificer of all things taught me, even wisdom' (7: 17–22).

So, in the mind of the author, natural knowledge, too, belongs to the sphere of religion, because the whole world is governed by divine wisdom. It is not true, then, as is so often taken for granted, that apart from its naïve description of the creation of the world at the very beginning, the Bible has no interest at all in the matters that today belong to the realm of science. Even though the Bible itself is not interested in transmitting scientific knowledge, because this is not its object, nevertheless it makes quite clear that the acquisition of such knowledge belongs to the authentic, divinely willed human activities.

There is an interesting story in the second chapter of Genesis, where God brings the various living creatures to man 'to see what he would call them; and whatsoever the man called every living creature, that was the name thereof'.

For in the view of the ancient Hebrews, as in that of some primitive peoples even today, the essence of a thing resided in its name. If a man knew the name of a thing he had power over it. So this story expresses the conviction that man has power over nature; he gives the other creatures their names, that is he knows what they really are and is himself superior to them.

Even in the opinion of the biblical authors, therefore, it is right that man should investigate nature, that his sense of wonder should explore the world in which he lives. If this is expressed in mythological rather than scientific language this is only to be expected at a time when the world of nature was still linked in man's mind with myths by which he tried to explain it. But the underlying conviction that nature is a legitimate field of man's enquiries was already there; and if Christians had paid more attention to these scriptural hints the unfortunate, one might

14

even say tragic, division between Christianity and science could have been avoided.

It is, however, an encouraging sign that scientists, as they discover more and more marvels, whether in the structure of the atom or in the universe, are beginning to regain the sense of wonder, which is the first step towards a more fully human conception of nature than the mere registration of phenomena. Because the universe is both intelligible to the human mind trained in scientific disciplines and yet so full of questions—regarding its origin, its duration, its extent and so forth—it seems that the sense of wonder will remain, however many new discoveries may be made.

But our human existence is not only made up of the phenomena of the world around us which are open to scientific investigation. It contains innumerable things about which science can tell us nothing, or very little. Science tells us that a rose, the Mona Lisa, a rat and a lovely young girl are all made up of colourless and scentless atoms. But it cannot tell us why we think the rose, the Mona Lisa, the young girl beautiful, whereas the rat is repulsive to most of us. Why does man respond in a certain way to colour, shape, scent, sound, how does it come about that his senses are attuned to the outside world? More, why will this response of man to his surroundings vary often in individuals, and even more in whole civilizations? Indeed, what is beauty? We all know instinctively what appeals to us as beautiful and what does not—but why is this so?

15

Beauty is one of those phenomena that do not impress all men or ages alike; it cannot really be defined, because it is an elusive quality, and if we are asked why we call something or someone beautiful, we shall be hard put to it to explain. It is quite true that beauty is largely in the eye of the beholder, yet there must be qualities in the object he contemplates that evoke his response: this is beautiful.

To explain this, Plato believed in a realm of ideas, where the archetypes of beauty, goodness, truth and so forth had an actual, separate existence of which their earthly realities were but a faint reflection. This realm of ideas is one of the philosophical myths which modern thinkers no longer accept; yet we cannot deny that these ideas do exist in the human mind, and it is difficult to see how they got there if we are nothing but a continuation of an animal.

Why are we attracted not only by physical, but also by moral beauty? Why do we admire a man who endangers his own life to save another's? There is certainly on scientific reason for it; for no scientist can prove why it should be better for a strong swimmer to endanger his life to save a weaker one, seeing that the law of nature decrees the survival of the fittest. Yet not even the most materialistically-minded atheist would dare say: more fool he.

For the strange fact is that all of us live by certain sets of values, even though some people's values may seem distorted to others; and these values can be neither proved nor disproved by scientific methods. For most of us act in accordance with what we believe is our moral duty, even though no sanctions may be attached to its opposite. We admire courage and despise cowardice, we esteem generosity and scorn meanness, we appreciate kindness and hate cruelty. It is difficult to account for all this sphere of aesthetic and moral awareness in man without the assumption of objective standards by which his conduct is—often quite unconsciously—ruled, even if his interpretation of these standards varies from age to age, from culture to culture.

Man stands in wonder before the world about him and before his inner world, summed up by the eighteenth century German philosopher Emmanuel Kant as 'the star-studded sky above me and the moral law within me', the immense universe of millions and millions of light years and the intangible values without which human life cannot be lived except, perhaps, on the very lowest level of the dehumanized criminal and the mentally deficient. And man's senses themselves are attuned to his surroundings; their impressions influence his inner life which reacts to them with pleasure or pain, with enjoyment or loathing, with eager anticipation or dreading fear. Thus man is inescapably linked to the outer world, yet he is not subject to it: he can both investigate it scientifically and let himself be moved by it morally and emotionally.

This moral and emotional reaction to his surroundings is strongest when it concerns his fellow-men. Here the reaction can take the form of friendship, affection, love, passion, or again of indifference, dislike or hatred. These varied emotions may be linked to the physical or moral characteristics of others; they will generally be affected by both, and, in addition, by some obscure attraction or repulsion for which we find it hard to account. These relations actually begin with birth and they cease only at death. Freud, the father of psychoanalysis, wanted to reduce them all to the sex instinct. This he believed to have discovered in the infant's turning to his mother's breast— though this seems to be far better explained by the instinct for food, itself based on the primal instinct for self-preservation.

True, the sexual instinct is one of the most powerful basic instincts, though, I should think, less universal than the instinct for self-preservation, and it influences our behaviour far more than the prudishness of the Victorian age would allow. But it is by no means at the basis of all our human relationships. There are many friendships based wholly on character or intellect—for example that of Dr Johnson and Boswell—and there are, both inside and outside Christianity, innumerable examples of noble men and women who cared personally for the poor and the sick, giving their whole life to them, activities which have really hardly anything to do with the sex instinct. We need only remember people like Florence Nightingale or the Abbé Pierre, Father Damien or Elizabeth Fry, to say nothing of the almost countless nurses, doctors, missionaries who give their lives for the relief of human suffering. We wonder at the tremendous power of love that animates such men and women, and which cannot be accounted for by any of the basic human instincts. What is at the root of such self-sacrificing impulse, which is something quite different from the easy philanthropy of the millionaire who writes large cheques for various charities?

It is surely a love for others, inspired not by any instinct but by a tremendous feeling of responsibility for one's fellow-men, something which may also be called conscience. It is not based on a powerful instinct like, for example, the mother's love that protects her child even at the risk of her own life, noble though it be. It is a wholly conscious love that springs from the conviction that all men, however different, are fundamentally brothers and bound to love and help one another. This love is precisely not based on instinct; rather, it runs counter to the natural re-actions to sickness, squalor, difference of race, class or customs.

There is a tendency today to run down, to 'debunk' even this noble love, to reduce it to psychological sublimations of lower motives. Of course, if one wants to run down all that is noble, all that seems to belong to a higher sphere than that in which our everyday lives are lived, it is quite possible to do so. But it does not for all that explain this higher form of existence. There is rather a sour grapes attitude about this debunking tendency: because we our-selves are not capable of such generosity and unselfish love we hate to admit that it exists in others. It is so much easier and more satisfactory to our self-esteem to admire the film star, the pop singer or the boxer to whom we do not feel inferior, because there is nothing intrinsically admirable in them and they do not call forth a deeper response of our being.

Not that film stars, pop singers, television 'personalities' have not their rightful place in our civilization. But what is rather frightening is that they should have usurped the position that has in former centuries been occupied by the 'heroes', the saints, the truly great men and women whose lives were animated by a higher ideal than to provide an hour's entertainment. Those great men appealed to the sense of wonder; their life reflected something that did not entirely belong to the natural sphere. Has 'modern man'—to use a much abused generalization—really lost his sense of wonder? Does he really reject everything that is called supernatural, that transcends his own sphere of being? Why, if this were the case, is he so interested in all forms of mysticism, in eastern religions, in experiments with drugs that promise to open up new horizons to his consciousness?

Surely these are signs that even contemporary man is not fully satisfied with a completely 'this-world' existence. And the very transitoriness of the fame of film stars and pop singers who are acclaimed one day and forgotten the next shows that there is a need for better and more lasting ideals. For what men have at all times wanted to discover in their heroes is a reflection of a higher power that was called divine, and which expressed itself precisely in a love, a goodness, a fortitude above that possible to 'ordinary' men and women and called forth the sense of wonder in them. So here again, in the human world, we meet something indefinable which seems to reflect, like the cosmos, something higher than either the world or man himself, though it is mirrored in both.

This 'reflection' may even appear in ordinary men in certain moments of their life. We may catch a glimpse of it in the sudden experience of an overpowering love that sweeps us out of ourselves, in hearing music, at the sight of a sunset or of a great painting, or in reading some passage in a book which suddenly gives us a flash of insight into a world that is quite different from our everyday surroundings. Every lover, every creative artist and many other men and women besides have had such experiences, however fleeting, that seemed to bring them into contact with something that appeared to belong to a world outside their normal experience, that called forth their sense of wonder in overpowering measure. Such experiences have at all times given a strong assurance to man that there is more behind this world than what appears to their senses and to their investigating mind, that this 'more' reflects a wisdom, a beauty, a goodness that is greater than both man and the cosmos. It is this power in and beyond the world that religious men have at all times called God.

The Transcendent God

'THE power in and beyond the world', is, in more
technical language, the God who is both immanent and
transcendent. It is a great pity that only too often, while
we grow up in all other ways, while we discard the images
of our childhood and no longer believe in forests peopled
with fairies and in Father Christmas climbing down the
chimney, we yet seem to retain religious imagery suited
only to the very young. Because we call God 'our Father in
heaven' we picture him as an old man dwelling in the sky;
because we have learned that he gives us commandments,
we think of him as a kind of headmaster doling out reports,
punishments and rewards. Indeed, he seems to us like a
superman, residing in an upper region, and it is apparently
not only in Russia that men feel they can no longer believe
in him because the astronauts did not meet him 'up there'

22

or somewhere 'out there' in space. There are even modern clergymen who hold that we must completely revise the Christian idea of God because it no longer fits what we know of the world.

But has this idea of God ever been held, either by the authors of the Bible or by the later Fathers and the great theologians of the Church? True, in the first chapters of Genesis we read about God walking in the garden and being sorry that he had created man. But these are stories fitted to a very primitive age when people, like children, could not yet grasp more abstract and exalted notions of the Godhead. As early as the eighth century before Christ the prophets of Israel taught a very different conception of God. For Isaiah, he was the Holy One of Israel, whose glory filled the earth, and a later writer in the same book warns the people that the thoughts and ways of God are infinitely higher than the thoughts of men.

In the New Testament the emphasis on the divine transcendence is even greater: the Father is invisible, he is spirit, and those who would worship him must do so in spirit and in truth. Now the concept of 'spirit' is very difficult; in the Old Testament it does not mean the immaterial principle such as the Greek philosophers developed it, but rather the breath of life. There are, however, certain indications that open up an approach towards the Greek conception, especially in a verse from Isaiah (31 : 3): 'The Egyptians are men, and not God; and their horses flesh, and not spirit', opposing the weakness and mortality of men and animals to the power of God who

will pass over and protect Jerusalem 'as birds flying'—
an image suggesting the elusiveness and mystery of
Spirit.

In the New Testament, Christ opposes the willingness of
the human spirit to the weakness of the flesh (Matthew
26 : 41) and, in the passage from St John's Gospel quoted
above, the adoring spirit of man is related to the adored
Spirit of God. Here spirit is conceived as the immaterial
principle, since it is coupled with truth. It means that God
is outside time and space; words like up, down, or even
within have no relevance when applied to him. Spirit is
something we cannot really comprehend; for we are in-
exorably tied to our bodies and thus to time and space;
even when we think of ourselves as having 'souls', as
Christians call the spiritual part of themselves, we cannot
really in our imagination separate these from our bodies,
in which we believe them to dwell. Unless we realize that
'spirit' is something of which we have no direct, first-hand
experience, we shall not be able to grasp what is meant by
the Christian idea of God.

Nevertheless, we all constantly make all kinds of statements about God. God is good, he is omnipotent, eternal,
just, wise, merciful and the like. But when Christians make
these statements, unbelievers immediately give many
examples why they must be wrong. What men see here on
earth, the sufferings, the injustices, the crimes—all this
cannot be harmonized with the idea of a God who is utter
perfection, as the monotheistic religions affirm. The very
difficult problem of the evil and suffering on earth will be

discussed in a later chapter; in this context it is relevant in a different way, as related to the divine transcendence. For even though we assign qualities to God which are also in men, we ought never to forget that we can do so only in an analogous way. This means that there is something in God that corresponds to our ideas of goodness, wisdom, power and the rest—but only corresponds, it is not identical with our ideas of these qualities. Human goodness, mercy, wisdom are always finite, relative, mixed with their opposites, they are never absolute, they can never even be imagined by us outside the context of our human life within time and space.

To take but one example. How can we ever judge a man with absolute justice? To do so we would not only have to know the innermost, even the unconscious impulses of a man, all his inherited traits, his exact strength and weakness of character, his childhood experiences, in fact all and everything that has contributed to make him what he is, we should also have to have a similar knowledge of ourselves, being able to discard completely all our own prejudices, complexes and what-have-you. Put in this way, it is surely obvious that no man can administer absolute justice to anyone. And even if we disregard for the moment all these psychological difficulties: which of us human beings knows what absolute justice is? For if, as Christians, we equate absolute justice with divine justice, we shall at once be confronted with the problem that in the unity of the Godhead justice is eternally linked to goodness, to power, to love, to all the other qualities of God, which in him are united, but which we can only consider separately, rather as the ray of light is broken into many colours in the rainbow, containing all these colours in itself, though we can only see them when the light is broken and reflected in drops of water.

It cannot be stressed often enough that this God to whom he speaks as his Father, completely transcends a man's understanding and imagination, however wise and clever he may be. When the apostles asked Christ, 'Show us the Father'; he replied that he who had seen him had seen the Father; in another passage he tells them that no one has ever seen the Father except himself, because he came from the Father; The Father of whom Christ speaks is the invisible God outside time and space, and his hearers understood this; they did not for a moment believe in an 'old man in the sky'; indeed, such an idea would have seemed either childish or blasphemous to them.

Nevertheless, when Christian theology developed during the first centuries of our era, some Fathers found it necessary to emphasize this transcendence, especially those who had themselves had mystical experiences. One biblical passage struck them particularly. It is the passage from the Book of Exodus (24 : 18) where Moses enters into a 'thick cloud' and there meets God. The darkness of this cloud symbolizes for them the transcendence and unknowability of God which a man experiences when he has made progress in the Christian life. Gregory of Nyssa, the great fourth century theologian of Cappadocia, writes in his life of Moses that in order to approach God a man must first completely strip himself of all preconceived ideas about him. For in this, Gregory teaches, consists the true knowledge of God, 'that he cannot be seen, because he transcends all knowledge, and is surrounded on all sides by his incomprehensibility as by a darkness'. God cannot be either imagined or understood, not because he is not intelligible in himself, but because the human intellect is simply not strong enough to apprehend him.

One of the most influential authors of the Greek Church rings the changes on this subject. He wrote under the name of St Paul's Athenian disciple Dionysius the Areopagite, but actually was a theologian of the end of the fifth century whose identity has remained a matter of controversy to this day. The pseudo-Dionysius, as he is usually called, wrote a treatise *On the Divine Names* in which he asserts that God can be known more surely by what he is not than by what he is. To express his total transcendence Dionysius invents a whole new vocabulary; he calls God 'the super-essential Indefinite', the 'unity that is beyond mind surpassing the mind', 'mind unintelligible and word unutterable'; he even calls God 'non-being', not, indeed, because he has no being, but because his being is infinitely superior to everything our human minds conceive as being. This manner of speaking of God in terms of what he is not rather than of what he is is the famous 'negative way' which has been used both by the mystics and by the professional theologians of Christendom throughout the ages in order to express the inexpressible, that is to say the absolute divine transcendence which the human mind simply cannot grasp, and which can therefore only be suggested by paradoxes.

We see how far removed this conception is from the old man in the sky, the God out there, up there or down there. For a God who transcends even the highest human concepts such as goodness, being and so forth can even less be localized in any way. This God is both within and outside the universe, precisely because space has no relevance to him. He is equally outside time, a fact known already to the author of Psalm 89 (90): 'for a thousand years in thy sight are as yesterday which is past'. Kant called space and time the forms of our perception; they belong to our human existence, they are not absolutes, they have no meaning in the divine sphere. It is very unfortunate for the Christian religion that no more emphasis is laid on this divine transcendence in the teaching of the young, once they are past childhood and have entered adolescence with all its questionings and criticisms. Christianity is only too often presented as 'having all the answers' and God as a being about whom we know a great deal, whose goodness, power, justice we can quite well understand. But a God whom we could understand would be no God; he would be no more than a kind of superman, a God made in our own image, whereas we are made in his.

This doctrine that man is made in the image of God, which we meet on the very first pages of the Bible, is also frequently misunderstood as making God somehow human. But it neither makes him human nor does it make us divine; it simply states a relationship between God and man which differs from that between the Creator and all his other creatures here on earth. For in order to understand a being higher than oneself there must be a certain affinity; the plant does not 'understand' the animal, nor do animals 'understand' men, while men have an adequate, even though imperfect, understanding of both plants and animals. And though God utterly surpasses human understanding, there is yet a sphere in men which can make contact with the Creator, the sphere of the 'image', which the mystics call by many names, such as the ground or the spark of the soul. If this sphere did not exist, men could not pray. Now prayer is an activity unknown to animals, but men have always practised it, from the most primitive fetish worshippers to our most sophisticated Christian contemporaries. For by prayer men acknowledge both a higher being, above their own human limitations, and the possibility of getting in touch with this being. If there were not an indestructible 'image' of the divine in man, he would live on earth without ever giving a thought to a higher being, much less trying to contact it.

Now many of our contemporaries may say: but we never pray—so what? But this is no counter-argument. There are many people who are by nature musical and yet do not know it, because through some circumstance or other they have never practised their gift but let it atrophy. Nevertheless, it is an observable fact that even men and women who never pray in ordinary circumstances will suddenly do so when in danger of death or otherwise in acute distress. This must surely mean that there is an instinct deep down in men that tells them that they are not alone nor wholly independent in the universe, that there is a power with whom something in themselves urges them to make contact. This is certainly not a mathematical proof for the existence of God but a psychological pointer towards it.

However, this divine power to whom these men turn can no longer be envisaged simply as a half-human father figure somewhere in the universe. For the universe itself has become de-divinized and de-humanized, while the nature we meet on earth has almost completely lost the mysterious, 'numinous' character it once had, so that the seventeenth century philosopher Spinoza could still speak of *Deus sive natura*, God or nature. As we come almost every day to know more about the secrets of nature in our solar system, as we increasingly learn to subject its forces to our needs, it is no longer awe-inspiring, it no longer fills us with religious emotions. At the same time there is no place for the divine in the immense universe of outer space either, however little we may actually still know about it.

The ancient Greek philosophers presumed that there were spheres round the earth, the highest of which was the seat of the gods, and much of popular Christianity, as opposed to the teaching of the Church and its theologians, still equated the 'sky above the stars' with the heaven of the New Testament. Because this was still possible for the uneducated even a century ago, the sudden loss of this image of the universe of which God was, as it were, a part, brought with it also a loss of God himself—and not only among the 'uneducated', but also among those educated in all other subjects except their religion.

But now the transcendence of God, the 'otherness' of him as opposed to the universe, which had been taught by the great theologians and experienced by the great mystics throughout the ages, simply has also to be discovered by all Christians, if they are not to give up their faith altogether. In the Middle Ages and even later, God's direct working was seen everywhere and men were ready to accept anything they could not understand as a miracle. Today we have learned far more about natural causation; from thunderstorms and aurorae boreales to trance states and the sudden cure of ulcers we no longer need to postulate direct divine causation. Even though the universe was made by God and is kept in being by him, he created it in such a manner that it has its own laws, which it follows, and he scarcely ever interferes directly with its running. Christians have for far too long been trying to refer anything they could not understand to direct divine action and have then had to retreat from one position after another as science has found a natural explanation, and this has made the Christian religion so unacceptable to many of our contemporaries.

Certainly, miracles, that is events outside the ordinary chain of cause and effect are not only possible, they do happen; but they are very few and far between; indeed, the very fact that there is no necessity for God to be all the time intervening in his world should strengthen rather

31

than weaken our faith. For what would we say if our watch or our television set were constantly out of order and needed the attention of watchmakers and engineers? It would be a very poor watchmaker, a very poor television factory that could not turn out instruments needing hardly any attention afterwards. The more perfect the knowledge and ability of the maker, the less need will there be for attending to what he has made. So we may well content ourselves with the fact that God has made the world in such a way that it is governed by its own laws, needing no outside intervention. It certainly takes away something of the 'cosy' religious feeling that we can no longer find him at every turn, sending thunderstorms and personally causing drought or rain; but it also makes him far more divine, far more 'God', who is precisely not the world, not behind every natural happening, but spirit infinitely transcending our petty notions. He is the tremendous and utterly inconceivable mind who has designed the universe but who has himself no place within it; there is no 'divine' sphere within the universe, and man has to resign himself to it.

The 'divine sphere' in the world is exclusively in man; he has to descend into himself if he would get into touch with the transcendent God, because the spirit of man in some way reflects the divine spirit: man was made in God's image, as the Genesis account says. This is the mystery which science can neither explain nor even affirm; it is outside its province altogether. For, strange though it may sound, the spirit of man itself transcends the universe in some way; it subjects at least a tiny part of it, according to the words of Genesis: 'And God created man to his own image . . . male and female he created them. And God blessed them, saying: Increase and multiply, and fill the earth, and subdue it.'

So the subjugation of the earth by his superior knowledge is part of man's vocation; it belongs to the divine image in which he was made. For man himself is creative, he was meant to be creative, this is part of his image relation to God. Religious people, who have often an instinctive fear of science and technology, have now retired to a position from which they assert that whatever else happens, at least man will never produce life. But scientists are already investigating this possibility; there is no *a priori* reason why they should not produce life very soon, and then another 'Christian' fortress will have fallen, and many will cry out, but if man can produce even life— what is left to God?

Again, these fears of religious people are due to an insufficient awareness of the divine transcendence. If man can produce living organisms from what is popularly called 'dead matter' this does not impinge on the divine prerogatives but only shows that hitherto we had not been sufficiently aware of the possibilities inherent in 'matter'. God does not cease to be infinitely above the mind of man simply because man has made yet another scientific discovery. For all his magnificent activities man remains in the sphere allotted to him, and even when he learns to create life, he will not create it out of nothing but only

33

transform what does already exist. In doing this he will not usurp divine rights but only fulfil his human destiny.

Many Christians are so terrified of new discoveries simply because their idea of God is insufficient. But the realization of his tremendous 'otherness', so clearly perceived by the Church Fathers and the great Christian theologians, is the best safeguard against such difficulties. It is a kind of thoughtlessness—as well as defective religious education—that makes so many Christians shy of acknowledging the divine transcendence in all its overpowering majesty. But if we cannot completely understand even another human being, even our most intimate friends, if we only too often are compelled to exclaim: 'I should never have thought it of him?', how can we pretend to understand God?

Therefore we shall have to resign ourselves more and more to the simple fact that the earth is the sphere where man works and is meant to work; it is also the sphere of evolution, as Teilhard de Chardin saw so clearly. It is part of man's worship of God that he should subdue the earth, that he should investigate the laws of nature, that he should experiment, even that he should split the atom and release its powers, for man was meant from the very beginning to be master of the earth.

That all these human activities, which are good in themselves, should invariably have bad side-effects is another matter; but this will be discussed in a later chapter. Because man's power over nature has increased so spectacularly in the last century it is absolutely essential that his conception of God should keep pace with human achievement; that is to say that the more exalted man seems to have become, the more exalted must be his conception of God. He simply can no longer be a God in some outer sphere, he must be acknowledged as the Being infinitely above the whole immense universe, the Spirit that is incommensurable with man and all that belongs to his world.

To many modern theologians the divine transcendence is unacceptable, because they refuse to conceive of God as a supernatural 'Being' and would bring him back into the world, calling him the 'ground of all being', 'the depth of experience', our 'ultimate concern' and similar vague expressions. But though these contemporary thinkers do not realize it, their 'new theology' is actually Spinoza's old 'God or nature' in modern dress. God is imprisoned in the world, he does not transcend it, hence he is part of the world. Their objection to a transcendent God is really an insufficient realization of what divine transcendence actually means. For it does not, as they affirm, enclose God, it does not make him a 'separate' being as one human person is separate from other human persons. The transcendent God is certainly separate from men, yet, through man being made in the image of God, he is also profoundly united to them. Neither the mistaken idea that traditional Christianity represents God as a kind of superman nor the modern view that he is no more than the 'ground of being' or the 'depth of experience' leave intact the 'otherness' of God which is the concern not only of the Fathers of the Church but also of a modern theologian like Karl Barth.

This 'otherness' is the reason why the great Christian thinkers speak so often in paradoxes when they are trying to express God in human terms, as they necessarily have to do. For they never lose sight of the fact that God is both infinitely above, and yet 'deep down' in, man; indeed, they leave intact the mystery of God and man.

If we once take the divine transcendence seriously, if we really no longer assume that God must be a kind of superman, our religion will become far deeper and far more genuine than if we try to visualize God somehow within our own terms of reference. This realization of the divine transcendence is bound to be a painful process, for we must abandon many notions and images that have become dear to us. But then all growth is painful, and spiritual growth most of all. It was none other than St Paul who wrote: 'When I was a child, I spoke as a child, I felt as a child, I thought as a child: now that I am become a man, I have put away childish things.' The Christian religion has for far too long been taught as if men were children; it is time that it should be taught now in an adult manner. And second in importance only to an awareness of the divine transcendence, an adult religion has to have an adequate notion of religious symbolism; for precisely because God is so utterly transcendent we can only speak of him by means of signs and symbols.

The Language of Religion:
Images and Symbols

In the preceding chapter the transcendence of God has been emphasized, and perhaps it may be asked how we can make any other than negative statements about God, if, as has been asserted, he cannot be grasped by human understanding. Now, however true it may be that human language is, strictly speaking, powerless to express anything about the transcendent God, man has nevertheless at all times endeavoured to make statements about him, and he has most often done so in images.

Speaking in images is by no means the preserve of religion. As we are bodies existing in space, our language is largely concerned with spatial imagery; we tend to express our most abstract thought in concrete pictures. The very term 'abstract' is not abstract at all but means 'drawn away'—a spatial image for a non-spatial notion. The spatial image of height may also generally be used to express superiority of any kind; we think at once of higher studies, higher education, higher mathematics, though no one would be so foolish as to imagine that these activities took place somewhere up in the air. If we consider that we do not understand a subject we say it is 'above' or 'beyond' us; we talk—or used to talk—about 'lower' classes; there is an upper and a lower sixth in schools. Further, a man's outlook may be 'broad' or 'narrow'—but again no one imagines that the outlook or the mind has spatial dimensions. The same applies to expressions like cold-hearted or warm-hearted, though the physical heart of the cold-hearted person has the same temperature as that of his warm-hearted neighbour.

Then there is the whole sphere of symbols. The lion is a symbol of strength, the eagle of swiftness; the colour red signifies love, whereas green stands for hope; a white flag means surrender, and a black veil is worn for mourning. The most abstract science of all, mathematics, is inconceivable without symbols, from the simple x as the unknown quantity in an equation to the most elaborate signs used in the intricate calculations of modern physics. Even our daily life is governed by symbols, and today more than ever before. They are so deeply embedded in our consciousness that we obey them without thinking: the motorist seeing a red light will stop instinctively; he will slow down when he sees a sign depicting two children, which tells him that he is near a school.

Examples of this use of images and symbols might be multiplied almost endlessly; we use them quite without thinking about them, because they come so naturally to us; and we all know perfectly well what they mean. It is therefore only to be expected that imagery will also be used in religious language; indeed, it will be used there more than anywhere else precisely because the subject is transcendent and cannot be explained—in so far as it can be explained at all—without the use of imagery. On the other hand, just because God is so utterly transcendent and unknowable in himself men will all the more easily be tempted to take the image for the reality. If we say that some difficult subject is 'above' us, we do not for a moment imagine that it is suspended above our heads. If we say God is 'above', there is a much greater temptation to visualize him somewhere in a region above the earth, especially as this 'above' is also expressed by the term 'in heaven', and as we are living in space we are immediately inclined to regard 'heaven' also as a part of space, albeit a 'higher' part.

Now as we have seen, the Greek philosophers actually thought that there was a sphere above the earth that was the abode of the gods; and in the earlier portions of the Old Testament also, God was somewhat localized: he dwelt above the ark of the convenant, in the Holy of Holies in the Temple, even though, being the Creator of the world, the whole universe belonged to him, while he himself was not part of it. Therefore he was pictured as 'above' it.

Nevertheless, this 'above' was rarely taken in a strictly local sense. For God who existed 'above' also spoke to

Moses 'as a man speaketh unto a friend', even though his transcendence is emphasized when he says that no man can see him and live. This twofold conception of God as both above man and with him in his own human sphere is particularly clearly expressed in many of the Psalms. For example in Psalm 121 (120) the author uses the strictly spatial metaphor of lifting his eyes to the mountains, when he prays to the Lord for help; but immediately afterwards stresses his nearness to man, calling him the shade (an image of protection) over the singer's right hand. In Psalm 108 (107) God is said to be exalted above the heavens, quite evidently a metaphor, and then asked to deliver his beloved people, for his glory is also 'above all the earth'. He is certainly not restricted to any particular sphere; the spatial imagery is used only to express his infinite superiority to his creation, to which he is nevertheless present.

Christ, too, when he spoke of heaven, was using imagery that was not meant to be taken in a local sense. This is quite clear when he says that 'the kingdom of heaven suffers violence' (Matthew 11 : 12) which it evidently could not do if it were 'up in the sky'. The non-local sense of the kindgom of heaven also emerges from the fact that in Luke's gospel it is generally called the kingdom of God, and as such is said to be 'within (or among) you' (17 : 21). Such instances could be multiplied; they show quite clearly that the spatial image of heaven is used to suggest the divine transcendence, not to assign a place to the divinity.

This transcendence, however, would seem to be made

more difficult to grasp by the presentation of God as a person, even as a father, since such language appears to endow him not only with personality in the human sense but also with sex. As we have seen, this conception of God is responsible for the imaginative picture of the 'old man in the sky'. But when Christ taught his followers the 'Our Father' he meant this father image to convey something very different. For the petitions that follow the address 'Our Father who art in heaven' show at once what the divine fatherhood is meant to express. The name of this divine Father is to be hallowed and his will is to be done on earth as it is in the transcendent realm that is called heaven; he is invoked as the giver of our daily bread, that is to say, in less popular language, as the being on whom our whole existence depends.

That he is called our *Father* does not imply sex but creative power and authority as well as love; indeed Christ himself, though a man, compared himself to a hen gathering her chickens under her wings (Matthew 23 : 37) to express his loving care for his people. It is difficult to rid ourselves of a mental picture of a man when we think of God as Father; on the other hand, without such a picture God would remain too vague—a 'God of the philosophers', as the seventeenth century French philosopher Pascal said, rather than the 'God of Abraham, Isaac and Jacob', the 'living God' who, through his love and paternal power, is intensely involved with man and man with him, as a father is involved with his children.

Moreover, in Christian theology the divine fatherhood is

41

seen as involving not only man, but God in himself. For he was Father from all eternity, even before the creation of the world, because he eternally generated his Son and with (or through, as the Eastern Church teaches) his Son he 'breathed' the Holy Spirit. Now this is a mystery which can be grasped only by faith, not by our limited understanding; it is mentioned here only to show that the words 'person' and 'father' when applied to God have a very different sense from those we give them in ordinary language; though, on the other hand, they do express something in the Godhead which, however faintly, corresponds to these human terms. It will perhaps become most clear how far removed the notion of 'person' in the deity is from what we mean by human person when we say that the Holy Spirit is the love between Father and Son, and is yet a person.

In human society love can only exist between persons, it cannot itself be a person, whereas in the perfect 'society' of the divine persons love itself is a person, because it belongs to the deity. And it is called 'person' in Christian theology because we cannot conceive of a being higher or more perfect than a person; but what this actually means in God surpasses our understanding. Thus also, when God is called our Father this does not restrict him to a masculine being; masculinity and femininity have no meaning in God, who is both above them and contains them in his being. Unless we realize again and again that these names we give to God are but human terms attempting to express the inexpressible, our religion will remain on a childish level and we shall probably find it increasingly difficult to reconcile it with our knowledge in other spheres.

The same applies to such expressions as 'on the right hand of God'. The authors of the biblical books knew as well as we do that God has no hands and that the directions right and left do not apply in the divine sphere. When therefore Stephen, the first Christian martyr, saw in his vision immediately before his death 'the Son of man standing at the right hand of God' this is but a picturesque form of speech indicating the closeness of the man Jesus to the deity. For again, right and left are but metaphorical expressions, the right side usually meaning the good, the left the bad side, just as in our political language right and left have assumed a quite definite meaning that has no longer anything to do with the actual directions.

The spatial imagery is used with special force when the biblical authors wish to express a particularly intense relationship between God and the world, and, above all, the incarnation. For here God really 'comes into the world'; 'he came into his own, and his own received him not'. But this is not a coming from outside, for 'he was in the world, and the world was made through him' (John 1 : 10). In Luke's account of the annunciation the angel is, indeed, represented as 'sent from God', but the actual incarnation is in no way described as God travelling through space, as is sometimes said. On the contrary, the mystery remains perfectly intact: when Mary had consented to bear a child 'the angel departed from her', and the reader is left with the impression that now Mary had conceived the Son of God—but how this happened he does not know, and there is certainly not the slightest suggestion that it involves any 'travelling' on the part of God; for even the Psalmists knew that the Lord is near (cf. Psalm 118 (119) : 151), the Creator has no need to 'travel' into his world, for he is present to man in his very being.

He is present to man—he is not identical with man, not even with the ground of his being, as some modern theologians have tried to interpret certain passages of St Paul (e.g. 1 Corinthians 2 : 12–16), and as some mystics, for example Master Eckhart, have described their overwhelming experience of union with God. Creature and Creator can never be the same, just as the artist is not identical with the work of art he has produced. We may, indeed, say that a man's whole spirit is in his work, yet we know perfectly well that this is a metaphorical way of speaking. And if the living man whose spirit is in the inanimate work he has produced transcends his work, how infinitely much more does the Creator God transcend his living creature, though his spirit can truly be said to indwell this creature. If we descend into the depths of ourselves we shall find God there—but we shall never be God. For all this imagery, be it of height or of depth, of without or within, is only the clothing with words of something that is beyond human understanding but that nevertheless can be reflected, as in a glass darkly, in our human language.

How far Christ himself went in using this image language can be seen in his parables. It is probably due only to our familiarity with them that we are not more astounded at his comparing the kingdom of heaven with such at first glance very unlikely things as a mustard seed or the leaven used for baking. But to make his points to these Oriental people who loved nothing so much as a good story, Jesus did not in the least object to comparing the most humdrum objects with the most sublime realities. He knew our human condition; he knew that man can be made to understand the supernatural only through the natural.

Perhaps the most striking of all his symbols and the one he used most frequently is that of the marriage feast. He liked to call himself the bridegroom, and to represent the timeless happiness of heaven as a wedding. For then as now a wedding was the occasion of intense rejoicing, and in Palestine in the time of Christ the bridegroom was responsible for supplying the wine on this occasion, as is clear from the account of the wedding at Cana (John 2 : 9f). This imagery was already used by the Old Testament prophets, especially Hosea, for the relationship between Israel and Jahweh, the bridegroom of the Chosen People. When Jesus used it with reference to his own person this was in itself an indication of his claim to divinity; he was the bridegroom of the New Israel, the Church, as Jahweh had been the bridegroom of the people of the old dispensation. What does this mean? First it must be emphatically affirmed that in Scripture this bridal imagery when applied to God or Christ and his people has no erotic, let alone sexual, overtones. It is employed for one purpose only, to express the permanent relationship of mutual and fruitful love. As the bridegroom cares for and protects his bride so God cares for and protects his people. Both are united by everlasting bonds. Marriage is the most intimate relationship possible between human beings; therefore it is made to serve as an image of the relation between God and man. While the image of the Father expressed love as well as authority, the image of the bridegroom added a tenderness, an intimacy which were lacking in the father image.

This tenderness, which was present already here and there in the Old Testament prophets, was tremendously enhanced through the incarnation; it appears especially in such images as the Good Shepherd and the Lamb. Jahweh was called the shepherd of Israel by the Psalmist: 'The Lord is my shepherd, I shall not want' (22 (23) : 1); Christ takes up this image and calls himself the Good Shepherd who lays down his life for his sheep (John 10 : 11) and in doing so becomes the lamb that is sacrificed for his people, as he appears in St John's gospel and in the Apocalypse. Everyone knows that Jesus was neither a shepherd nor a lamb—these, again, are images to express certain religious truths about the relation between Christ and his people. But, as Dionysius the Areopagite rightly says, it is easier to abstract from imagery and turn towards the reality it is meant to represent when the imagery is completely inadequate, that is when Christ is represented as a lamb, or a hen with her chickens, or when Jahweh is called a lion.

Everyone understands quite easily that these are simply pictures representing certain aspects of the divine, we do not try to visualize Christ as a hen or God as a lion. But when it comes to human imagery it is far more difficult to abstract from the image, because man has, indeed, something in common with God in his spiritual being, and therefore tends to forget that if God is represented as a person, a father or a bridegroom, this, too, is image language and simply meant to express some aspect of his being which, owing to the poverty of man's language and understanding, can only be expressed in such human terms.

Besides image language there is also the language of gestures. When Christ prayed he raised his eyes to heaven, when the publican (Luke 19 : 13) prayed he did not dare to do this, but prayed with his head bent. These gestures do not mean that God is somewhere up in the atmosphere or, in the latter case, below the worshipper's head—they are simply meant to symbolize the raising of one's heart to God—though God is everywhere—and the acknowledgement of one's unworthiness, respectively. Praying with one's hands stretched out—as was the custom in Christian antiquity—or with them folded, with one's eyes closed, standing or kneeling are all meant to express different attitudes, a going out towards God, concentration, respect, humility, even though all these attitudes may be present just as much without being expressed externally. But here on earth man exists in the body, not outside it, and so he must express himself by means of the body. Christ certainly did not believe the God he called his Father was a man somewhere up above the clouds—yet, in his prayer he used the symbolism of the 'above' and raised his eyes to heaven.

It is an extraordinary phenomenon that so many of our

contemporaries will not credit the authors of the Bible with the capacity of distinguishing between the symbol and what it is meant to express; it is thought they really meant to confine God to a certain space 'up there' or 'out there', simply because they used the image language indispensable to ordinary men if they would express transcendence. It is, of course, true that the Jews and the early Christians had a different conception of the universe from that of our time; yet in their emphasis on the otherness and the mystery of the 'world beyond' they made it sufficiently clear that they, followed by the later Fathers and theologians, did not think in terms of physical space and time when it was a question of the eternal world.

Unfortunately, insufficiently instructed people have often misunderstood the teaching of the Old and New Testaments in this way, and especially that of the apocalyptic books. For there imagery runs riot, as it were, because it is a case of visions of 'the world to come' which could be presented to the visionary only in terms of earthly imagery, just as the later Christian mystics were unable to express their experience other than in human language, though they constantly affirm that the actual experience is inexpressible. If, therefore, the apocalyptic authors write of strange animals, of cities made of gold, jasper, emerald and the like, all these things have to be taken as descriptions of the indescribable, visions of supernal beauty for which human language is totally inadequate.

For Eastern men even now image language is immediately understandable: whereas we in the West have learned for centuries to think in abstracts, and even where we necessarily use images we are hardly aware of doing so —as in our use of 'above', 'below' and the like. But the Hebrews thought in images all the time; they did not know and use the abstract language of philosophy as did the Greeks. When the young Christian Church conquered the Hellenistic world it came into contact with this philosophy, and the early Christian Fathers had to translate the imagery of the Bible into a new and much more abstract idiom. This was no easy task and it often produced controversies, but these were finally settled at the great Councils, and new definitions were formulated to express biblical truths in language understandable to people brought up in traditions different from those of the ancient Hebrews.

Today theologians once more try to go back behind these formulas and understand the Bible as far as possible in the way it was understood by the authors of its various books themselves. And because the Hebrew authors used so much imagery, we now begin to realize that their meaning is often far more comprehensive than can be expressed by a philosophical formula. The formula is not false, but it is rather like a skeleton: it gives the essential, it rules out actual error, but it is not the living, many-coloured reality that shines forth through the scriptural imagery. Thus the Christological formula of the Council of Chalcedon (451 A.D.), that Christ was a divine person but had two complete natures, one divine, the other human, united in this divine person, told Christians the abstract truth about the phenomenon of Christ, but if we

49

would really know him and come into personal contact with him we have to go to the gospels, which present a living picture of this mysterious man who is called there by such strange and various names as Son of God, Son of Man, Lamb, Shepherd and Word.

The Phenomenon of Christ

THOUGH we have discussed the fact that religious truth must be expressed by images, we have not so far analyzed the image par excellence, the image of God which is Christ, as St Paul states repeatedly, for example in his Second Letter to the Corinthians (4 : 4) and in Colossians 1 : 15.

Nevertheless, Christ is 'image' in a very different sense from that in which we have used the word before. In the case of all the other images there were only certain traits corresponding to the reality they were meant to express: the Lamb was meant to show the sacrificial aspect of the life of Christ, the father image made the relationship between God and his creatures more understandable, the spatial metaphor of 'above' expressed the divine superiority and transcendence. But Christ, the incarnate Son of the divine Father is his perfect and wholly adequate image, so much so that Jesus could say: 'He who has seen me has seen the Father'. He is God really visible and tangible; he does not just reflect one aspect of the divinity, he does not merely call God to mind, he is his image in the sense of being identical with him: 'I and the Father are one' (John 10 : 30), and he claimed for himself the eternity of the Godhead: 'Before Abraham was, I am' (John 8 : 58).

Now these are very difficult sayings, and they were as difficult for Christ's contemporaries as they are for many of us. For they meant nothing less than an explicit claim to divinity, and the man who made it ate, drank, slept and generally lived exactly like other men, except that he did miracles—but then the Old Testament prophets had done miracles and yet never claimed divine status. True, many modern critics assert that Christ himself never made such a claim; that it is to be found only in St John's gospel, which is later than the three others, generally called the Synoptists, and that it can therefore not be considered authentic.

But this is not quite correct. In the Sermon on the Mount Jesus places explicitly his own authority above the authority of Moses. 'You have heard that it was said to the ancients . . . but I say to you'. Now the Jews believed that Moses had received the Law from God himself; therefore anyone who interpreted this law in an entirely new and authoritative way which really changed its meaning while yet fulfilling it in an unheard-of manner claimed implicitly, by this very fact, divine authority. His hearers were not slow to grasp this implication of his teaching: their comment was that he taught as one having authority and not as the scribes and Pharisees—though these certainly claimed to be the accredited teachers of Israel.

This superhuman authority is reflected also in the attitude of the people to Jesus. The centurion believes firmly that his servant will be healed by a mere word from Jesus, Christ himself claims repeatedly the power to forgive sins —definitely a divine prerogative and regarded as such by the scribes, that is to say by the Jewish theologians of the time, who consider this claim a blasphemy—so Jesus confirms it by doing a miracle. The very fact that he calls himself the bridegroom, which, as we saw, was a favourite term for Jahweh, is further evidence that he identified himself with the God of Israel. The disciples themselves, as well as many others who came into contact with Jesus, also realized that there was another side to this 'carpenter's son' who lived among them seemingly like other men, a side which they could not understand and from which they instinctively shrank. When the disciples saw Jesus walking upon the waters they cried out with fear, thinking he was a ghost. When, at Christ's command, they took a miraculously large draught of fishes Peter knelt in fear before him saying: 'Depart from me, for I am a sinful man'. At the transfiguration too, when, shortly before the passion, Jesus showed himself in his glory, his face shining and his clothes white as light, the apostles who witnessed it were struck down with fear and fell on their face. Even when he healed men by driving out devils, those who witnessed the event were frightened, realizing that here was a mysterious power which they could not understand and which, however beneficial, they would rather not have too near them; so they asked him to leave the district. Again, when he stilled the storm on the lake the disciples were frightened; this authority over the forces of nature which he so easily exercised was something superhuman, that terrified them and made them wonder who he really was, this young rabbi, 'that he commands both the winds and the sea and they obey him'.

For the Jesus that emerges from the Gospels is someone very different from the 'meek and mild', milk and water person he is often represented as in popular hymns and pictures. True, he gave himself to men as an example of meekness and humility, but in him these qualities had nothing soft. To be able to turn the other cheek a man must have a very strong personality, a will capable of subjecting the violent instinctive reactions of the self. Moreover, everything depends on the situation in which we find ourselves. To offer no resistance when we ourselves are wronged is one thing; the attitude demanded by Christ when the rights of God or our neighbour are violated is quite another. He himself drove the money changers out of the temple, and he did not hesitate to attack the Pharisees in the strongest terms because their ideas about religious observance laid intolerable burdens on men, though he was well aware of their powerful hostility which would finally lead to his own death.

A man who was nothing but 'meek and mild' would

never have appeared so dangerous to his countrymen that they could feel safe only when he was dead; but the religious authorities of Jerusalem recognized only too clearly that here was a power completely dwarfing their own, hence he had to be silenced for ever. That just this act of silencing Jesus was destined to result in the spread of his authority far beyond Palestine and throughout future ages is one of the great paradoxes of Christian history.

The call of the apostles, which follows the first chapters of Matthew from which the preceding examples have been taken, is yet another proof of Christ's own consciousness of his divine powers. For he commanded them not only to preach, but gave them authority to cast out devils and to heal diseases—powers which no human being can confer upon others even if he should possess them himself. More, he told them that to be worthy of him they must love him more even than their father and mother—a tremendous demand, especially in view of the great honour in which the Jews held their parents, in accordance with the fourth (fifth) commandment. Such instances could be multiplied; they all show quite clearly that Christ himself demanded an unconditional surrender to his person such as only an insane dictator or a divine Being could ask from his followers.

Now, although enraged enemies of Christianity have sometimes accused Christ of madness, even non-Christians, whether Mohammedans or modern neo-pagans, have always honoured him as one of the greatest and wisest guides of mankind. Nevertheless neither Mohammed himself nor Confucius or Lao-tse have ever made the demands Christ made, never claimed that their disciples must leave all and attach themselves totally to their own person.

Naturally, all these considerations are not philosophical, let alone scientific, proofs of the divinity of Jesus Christ. If this could be proved to the complete satisfaction of human reason men would believe in Christ as they believe that twice two are four. But, taking into account all the evidence from Scripture and from Christian history—which will be discussed presently—it may well gain the assent of what Newman called the 'illative sense', that is the 'power of judging and concluding', the only 'ultimate test of truth and error in our inferences'. We can infer that Christ was God from the phenomenon as presented in the New Testament and the later developments in the course of Christianity—we cannot prove it either by philosophical or scientific methods.

But between the life and claims of Christ as presented in the gospels and his emergence in the history of the Church there lies an event that is, indeed, the most crucial of all and on which Christians have ever claimed their faith to be based. It is the resurrection of Christ, followed by the outpouring of the Holy Spirit, that changed the timid fishermen who had fled at the crucifixion into fearless apostles ready to die for the man who had taught them and lived with them for less than three short years of their life. The evidence for the resurrection is about as good as that for any other event in antiquity, being described in various ways in the gospels, having as its foundation the discovery of the empty tomb by some pious women and after them by the apostles Peter and John. This discovery was followed by the appearance of Jesus to his disciples.

Now the strange thing about these resurrection appearances is that in some of them the disciples did not recognize Jesus. In Luke's gospel the two disciples who were on their way to Emmaus thought he was a stranger until they realized his identity at the moment when he broke bread with them as he had done at the Last Supper; in St John's gospel Mary Magdalen mistook him for a gardener; the disciples did not know who he was when he spoke to them from the shore of the lake; besides, Thomas was so sceptical that he would not believe the others who had seen him until he had himself touched his wounds with his own hands. In Mark's gospel it is explicitly stated that Christ appeared in different forms, and that those disciples who had not seen him yet did not believe the others who had. Just these variances and difficulties in the resurrection story make it ring much more true than if there had been one coherent narrative stating that the risen Christ appeared to his followers in unmistakable glory so that they were immediately convinced of the reality of the resurrection.

Why should the evangelists have caused just this decisive narrative to bristle with difficulties unless what they told was exactly what the apostles had experienced? Why should they admit that Christ had been mistaken for a stranger or a gardener, an error which must discredit the apostolic witness rather than make it more acceptable? Instead of describing a unique, overwhelming experience, *mysterium tremendum*, the authors of the gospels speak about it in everyday language and make no efforts to weld the different reports that circulated into a consistent whole. It is just this ambiguity and divergence of the descriptions that make them so much more credible than a consistent story.

The one fact on which all the narratives agree is the empty tomb. Much has been written about it, but it has never been explained. For the tomb was obviously guarded—so how could the apostles have removed the body? And even if this explanation were accepted, is it psychologically possible that this fraud should have changed the timid disciples who had fled like cowards when Christ was arrested into the heroic martyrs prepared to undergo every torture and death for the same Christ whom they had abandoned in his hour of need? Surely something that changed the situation completely must have happened between the crucifixion of Christ and Peter's fearless preaching recorded in the Acts of the Apostles. Is it so utterly absurd to accept what the New Testament authors tell us, that this strange teacher and miracle worker from Galilee really did conquer death and after his crucifixion lived on earth for forty days to strengthen his disciples for the work that lay before them, until he finally left them?

It would be absurd, had nothing further happened. But

the extraordinary sequel of this short life of a Jewish rabbi is the Christian Church, which in the two thousand years of its history has transformed the Western hemisphere and produced new cultures and an entirely new way of life, which still continues to influence even those who reject the doctrinal claims of Christianity.

For the strange fact is that ever since the death and resurrection of Christ he has exercised the most profound influence on the personal life of millions of men and women. They did not just accept his teaching, but developed an intense devotion to his person which permeated their whole existence. Whether we think of Paul of Tarsus or St Augustine, of Francis of Assisi or John Wesley, of St Gertrude or Teresa of Lisieux, of a militant reformer like Luther or a thinker like Blaise Pascal—all true Christians, great or small, men or women, simple people or scholars, have always lived their Christian life in an intense relationship with Christ as a living person, with whom they are convinced to be in intimate contact.

St Paul's watchword was 'in Christ'. According to him we have been buried with Christ in baptism and have risen again with him to a new life, which is nourished by the eucharistic bread and wine, which are the body and blood of Christ into whom we are incorporated through these sacraments, so much so that the apostle could write: 'Now you are the body of Christ.' For what is called the 'sacramental system' of Christianity exists solely for the dual purpose of bringing Christians into the closest personal relationship with Christ, believed to be a living being, both divine and human, and therefore capable of entering into the innermost part of men, and through him into communion with one another.

This entering in, this union between Christ and Christians, is not an imaginary experience of some highly emotional men and women. It has a spiritual reality which shows itself in the whole life of those who take it seriously. True, there are millions of Christians for whom their religion is not much more than a variety of external observances. They have, indeed, been buried with Christ in baptism and are nourished by the eucharist, but as they have not opened their whole being to his influence, Christ does not really 'live' in them. He himself taught that the religious seed he had come to sow would indeed reach many, but that it would grow and bear fruit only in a comparatively small number of those to whom it had come. So the scandal of lukewarm or even vicious Christians is indeed a scandal, but it is no argument against Christianity. The sacraments do not work by magic. Even though a man is 'incorporated' into Christ by baptism, that does not mean that he is already 'another Christ'; unless he realizes this incorporation 'existentially', to use a rather hackneyed term of modern philosophy, it will remain a mere formality, without any effects on his personality.

If, however, a person really opens himself to the influence of Christ, the most amazing transformations may take place. Church history is full of them, from the persecutor Saul who became the apostle Paul, to the reckless pianist, gambler and man-about-town Hermann Cohen who, as the Carmelite Father Augustine Mary of the Blessed Sacrament founded the church and community of his order in London. But even more extraordinary than the conversions of individuals is the transformation of the Western world which was brought about by nothing other than the phenomenon of Christ. For beside the personal union of Christ with the believer in the sacrament of holy communion there is, as St Paul never wearies of affirming, the union of believers with one another in what the apostle calls the 'Body of Christ'. For Christianity is essentially a social religion, aiming at uniting men not only to God but to each other, according to Christ's own prayer: 'That they may be one' (John 17:11). St Paul worked out this union in his teaching on the Church, the community of Christians, as the Body of Christ. This community is, as it were, the extension of Christ's person in time and space, reaching into future ages and far-away countries.

As the physical human body, so the Body of Christ is a unity in diversity: its different members have different offices, yet all are directed from one centre, the head, just like the ordinary human body. And because they are so directed, they are a unity which cannot be broken; Christ himself used a different image, to express the same thing, in his metaphor of the vine and its branches, through which the same sap flows.

The community of Christians in the unity of its head is, of course, an ideal; it is the image of the community as it ought to be according to the design of God. It looks very differently in its earthly actuality, because of the imperfection of our existence on earth, marred by the defects of evolution and the evil that is bound up with this existence. But the design is there and is still recognizable, as an artistic design is still visible even in a faulty execution by an incompetent craftsman. Thus, despite all its faults, we can still recognize the community-building design of the 'Body of Christ' in Christian history.

When the barbarian Germanic tribes invaded the Roman Empire in the fourth and fifth centuries of our era, Italy, then together with Byzantium the centre of European civilization, would have collapsed completely had it not been for the resistance of the Church, which finally succeeded not only in converting but in civilizing the invaders. The so-called Dark Ages between the sixth and tenth centuries, though devoid of outstanding scholars and artists, are nevertheless a period of slow cultural gestation, when the monks of St Benedict taught the newly converted pagans agriculture and the rudiments of civilized living and preserved the classical and patristic authors from being lost by assiduously copying manuscripts.

Thus, between the twelfth and the fourteenth centuries Western Europe witnessed an amazing flowering of scholarship, art and dedicated life: St Thomas Aquinas wrote his immortal *Summa Theologica* in which he synthesized the newly discovered Aristotle and the medieval Jewish (Moses Maimonides) and Arab (Avicenna) thinkers with the tenets of the Christian faith;

62

St Francis of Assisi inspired whole generations with his ideal of Christian poverty and charity; Wolfram of Eschenbach wrote his Christian epic of Parsifal and the Grail; cathedrals arose that were dreams in stone and stained glass, like Chartres; and in convents and monasteries men and women lived lives of close union with Christ, the contemplation of whose sufferings and glory filled their existence. For devotion to his person was at the root of the whole medieval civilization. This does not mean that this civilization did not have grave faults. Superstition was rife, side by side with deep faith, and despite spectacular personal charity the social conscience was hardly developed. Yet the impact of Christ's person alive in the Church had transformed the Europe of savage tribes into a community with high ideals and magnificent achievements.

This impact was not lost when the unity of Christendom broke down in the Reformation; for intense devotion to Jesus remained the hallmark also of most of the new communions, be they Church of England, Lutheran, Presbyterian or others. The strangest phenomenon, however, is that the influence of Christ continues even in those who have repudiated any form of Christianity.

In pagan antiquity there was no question of the fundamental equality and rights of men. Slaves were considered no better than cattle; the insane were treated even worse; baby girls and maimed children were often left untended to die of starvation. All our social institutions today are in the last resort an outcome of Christ's teaching on the duty to love our neighbour in whatever form he may be presented to us, even if he be our enemy. True, Christians have often been far from obeying this command of their Lord, but that it should have penetrated so deeply into our civilization that it is recognized and acted upon even by those who reject the divinity of Jesus Christ and refuse to be called Christians is surely a fact that ought to give us food for thought. All the social institutions which we are taking for granted today: hospitals, orphanages, old age homes, the Red Cross organizations, widows' pensions, unemployment benefit and the rest are known only to those civilizations that have received the impact of Christianity in one form or another.

True, this influence of Christ may sometimes be checked. The German nineteenth century philosopher Friedrich Nietzsche proclaimed the revaluation of all values and rejected the Christian care for the weak, Christ's own example of mercy and gentleness, by setting up the ideal of the ruthless 'Superman', the 'blonde beast', which in our own time the Nazis attempted to actualize. The very horror this neo-pagan philosophy inspired in most Western nations is sufficient proof of how deeply the person of Christ has influenced our whole outlook.

I say his person, not his teaching, advisedly. For many wise men, Socrates and Plato among them, taught a noble way of life, yet their teaching never penetrated whole civilizations; it remained the preserve of a few, and their persons remained buried in text books, never coming to life in millions upon millions of human hearts.

This is the mystery of Christ: that he lives not only in those called by his name, but that his influence extends very powerfully even to those who do not accept him as their master. It is sometimes said, and not without reason, that certain non-Christians are far more 'Christian' than those who profess to be Christians. These non-Christians frequently call themselves 'humanists', because they assert that they are interested only in men, not in God. But where did they learn their compassion and love for their fellow-men? In fact, whether they admit it or not, they did not learn it from anyone else but Christ, who told men to love their neighbour as much as they loved themselves and to do good even to those who persecuted them.

This tremendous influence of Jesus, the carpenter's son of the insignificant little town of Nazareth in the equally insignificant little Roman province of Judea is a fact very difficult to account for. Christians have always explained it by the fact of the resurrection, which convinced them that Jesus was really the Son of God, as he himself had affirmed. It certainly seems that this explanation is at least not less convincing than any other that non-Christians might think up.

The Teaching of Christ

Mᴜᴄʜ lip service is paid both by Christians and others to the moral teaching of Christ expressed particularly in the Sermon on the Mount. Today exegetes of all denominations are agreed that this is not a sermon that was actually preached, but a collection of sayings pronounced on various occasions and strung together by the author of St Matthew's gospel or of its source. These sayings concern very different subjects; they are by no means a kind of textbook of morality; many are expressed in paradoxical form so as to strike their hearers as forcefully as possible: hence a certain amount of interpretation is necessary if they are to be rightly understood.

The sermon begins with the so-called beatitudes, which are a kind of programme of the 'revaluation of all values', to use Friedrich Nietzsche's formula for his own philo-

sophy. Christ does not call blessed those who lead a pros-
perous and successful life, but the poor and those who
mourn, 'because they will be comforted,' that is to say
because they are not attached to earthly goods and so are
the better able to appreciate the spiritual riches of the
kingdom of heaven. The following beatitudes all praise
characteristics not usually valued by those anxious to get
on in the world: blessed are the meek, those that hunger
and thirst after righteousness, the merciful, the pure in
heart, the peacemakers and, last of all, those who are
wrongly persecuted and reviled.

Sometimes these Christian qualities of meekness, mercy
and purity of heart are presented as something negative,
an absence of strength and vigour. But neither meekness
nor purity come easily to most men; they have to be
acquired by a long struggle against their lower instincts.
As to the peacemakers: we all know how very difficult
it is to reconcile enraged enemies, be they individuals
or nations; it happens only too often that both parties
turn against those who would make them abandon
hostilities.

And what is more difficult and requires more strength
of character than to endure persecution? We have seen in
our own time how those outwardly 'strong men' who
persecuted and tortured others in the Nazi concentration
camps broke down and committed suicide when they
themselves were about to be punished far less cruelly than
their victims. In the beatitudes Christ praised strength,
not weakness, a spiritual strength capable of overcoming

even physical force, that has been put to the test time and again in the history of Christianity.

Nor did Jesus tell his followers to hide themselves and flee from 'the world', that is to say from their fellow-men. On the contrary, he told them that they were 'the light of the world' and should let this light shine before men and so bring them to God. In the following centuries many fervent Christians believed that to lead a truly Christian life they had to withdraw from the world into the desert and live as hermits. On the face of it this would seem to be in flat contradiction with Christ's command to let their light shine before men, but strangely enough it was just these lives of the solitaries in the desert that attracted the greatest admiration in the ancient world so that hundreds and thousands of men flocked to the famous hermits to ask their advice and benefit from their example.

In the following sections of the 'sermon' Jesus expounds in what way his own teaching differs from that of the ancient Jewish law.

In modern times this idea that Christ gave a new law, opposed to the Mosaic law, has been vigorously attacked. But it depends on what we mean by 'law'. It is quite true that the Sermon on the Mount does not legislate for particular situations but only gives broad principles, and these in language which is far removed from intricate legal definitions. But it is open to question whether the 'new law' has ever been regarded as anything else. Throughout almost two thousand years of Christianity men have neither cut off their hands nor plucked out their eyes—we shall see presently what Christ really did mean by these sayings. It is nothing new—as the representatives of the 'new theology' seem to think—that such commands cannot, and were not meant to be, taken literally. Nevertheless, while admitting this, it cannot be said that Christ never meant to give 'prescriptive' laws. Christ in his humanity was a Jew, and as he himself said he came not to destroy but to fulfil the Jewish law. He not only accepted unquestioningly the Ten Commandments but, as will be seen, he interpreted them in such a way as to make them very much harder to obey than they were in their original formulation. He would certainly not have subscribed to the statement of Bishop Robinson, following certain German religious thinkers, that 'nothing can of itself always be labelled as "wrong" '. It is very difficult to see how, for example, murder or adultery could be right in one case and wrong in another. There may, indeed, be extenuating circumstances in certain cases, but this does not make such actions right in themselves.

Moreover, Christianity is not so much concerned with what is morally wrong as with sin, and though these will in most cases coincide, they are not identical. For to call an action wrong is to judge it by human standards of morality, whereas sin is an offence against the standards set by God himself, and therefore also to be judged by him. Sin is a matter between God and the individual, it is the individual's falling short of the divine commandment. Christ came to call sinners and to bring them God's forgiveness—he never suggested that the sins he forgave might not really be sins in themselves, that is to say objective wrongs committed against his Father, against the laws he had given them—and not only against those given to Moses on Mount Sinai, but also against the law which, as St Paul writes in his letter to the Romans, is written in man's heart, 'their conscience bearing witness . . . and their thought . . . accusing or else excusing them' (2 : 15).

Both Christ and St Paul knew human nature far too well to imagine that men could live without laws, even in their redeemed state. If nothing could ever be labelled wrong by itself, conscience would have no objective standard by which to be guided, and no man would acknowledge himself a sinner, because he would always be able to find excuses for whatever he had done wrong.

Certainly, love is at the centre of Christian morality, and St Augustine said 'Love, and do what you will'. But the great difficulty of man as he exists at present is that he finds it extremely hard to distinguish between love in the Augustinian sense, which is the highest form of Christian charity, and his own emotions, which may be something quite different. It cannot be repeated too often that for Christ himself, as opposed to our 'new' theologians, the commandments were not dissolved by love, but the authenticity of love was judged by obeying the commandments: 'If you love me, you will keep my commandments' (John 14 : 15). These 'commandments' can, indeed, be summed up in the twofold commandment of love of God and one's neighbour, but Jesus himself did not hesitate to give them a more concrete form in his own interpretation of the Ten Commandments. And his interpretation in the Sermon on the Mount is really in many ways surprisingly modern.

For today we hear much about depth psychology: to understand why men behave as they do we have to find out the secret, often unconscious springs of their actions. Now Christ is not satisfied with outward action; he looks to its motivations. Not that he has anything to say about the unconscious—that is not the sphere of the religious teacher, because it is not subject to the human will. What he asks of his followers is to transform their inner attitude towards their fellow-men, from which their external actions develop. Thus, killing is the effect of hatred and anger and these must be overcome even if they should not lead to actual killing, because they poison one's whole character. A man's neighbour is as much a child of God as he is himself, hence before he performs any act of religious worship he should first be reconciled to his fellow-men; otherwise his worship will be a mockery.

The same holds good for the prohibition of adultery. It is not enough to refrain from the act, no, 'every one that looketh on a woman to lust after her hath committed adultery with her already in his heart'. This does not, of course, condemn any first spontaneous desire, but the deliberate dwelling on imaginary pleasures which, again, will poison the relation between man and woman. Therefore Jesus uses a highly paradoxical expression to enforce his teaching: 'If thy right eye causes thee to stumble, pluck it out and cast it from thee . . . and if thy right hand causeth thee to stumble, cut it off, and cast it from thee.'

These sayings do not counsel self-mutilation; neither the right eye nor the right hand will actually cause a man to stumble. They are only picturesque expressions in the Oriental manner inculcating that a man must be quite ruthless in removing the causes of sin.

But does not this teaching flatly contradict modern psychology, which tells us that it is dangerous to suppress our desires because such suppression will inevitably lead to neuroses?

It is quite true that we owe many valuable insights to psychoanalysis and depth psychology in general. But if we were to apply indiscriminately the famous teaching that the suppression of instincts leads to neuroses we would all have to go back to the jungle. For from early childhood our whole education tends to the suppression of many of our instinctive reactions. The mother who tells her eldest to share his toys or sweets with his younger brother or who forbids him to push his little sister would be producing neurosis, the schoolboy who has to study when he would prefer to be playing would be in danger of acquiring one, the young man or woman who must work in an office when he or she would much rather be sailing or playing tennis would be injuring their mental health.

It simply is not true that the suppression of our instincts or, in more old-fashioned terms, self-control, leads to neuroses. On the contrary, it is a fact of experience that very often just those people who have everything they want and who deny themselves nothing are the most likely subjects of nervous disorders. Men are not animals; they are capable of being guided by reason, and just this capacity to follow their superior powers rather than their lower instincts makes them fully developed, mature human beings.

When Jesus, therefore, told his disciples to pluck out an eye or cut off the hand that caused them to stumble, this was no more than a metaphorical way of saying that they must control their bad instincts at all costs, however difficult they may find it. The somewhat inhuman-sounding imagery he uses to inculcate this moral necessity only serves to drive home his point; it is not at all an incentive to self-mutilation. For in our interpretation of biblical stories and sayings we have always to allow for a mentality different from our own Western way of thinking and expressing ourselves. Where we would speak in abstracts the Oriental uses concrete terms, where we would argue, the Eastern man tells a story.

And so the teaching of Jesus, too, is largely conveyed by stories or parables, as is the technical term for them. These stories are brief, pithy narratives, mostly taken from the daily experience of his hearers. Many of them convey a definite teaching on what human behaviour ought to be like. Such is the famous parable of the good Samaritan, who helped the wayfarer who had been robbed and wounded, at considerable expense to himself, while the priest and the Levite, the representatives of official

Jewish orthodoxy, passed by without taking any notice of the man in need. Now the Samaritans were hated and despised by the Jews as 'heretics', because they did not keep strictly to the law of Moses and certain elements from the surrounding pagan cults had infiltrated into their worship. Precisely by setting up a Samaritan as an example of neighbourly love, Jesus took the concept of charity out of a narrow nationalistic-orthodox context and made it universal. Not only does every man, whether friend or foe, have a right to help when he is in need, but whoever practises this charity, whether he be orthodox or heretic, fulfils the divine law of love.

This teaching is repeated even more forcefully in the description of the Last Judgement, when the righteous will be separated from sinners according to their behaviour to those in need, who represent Christ himself. For, he says 'as long as you did it to one of the least of my brothers, you did it to me'. Or, in the words of one of the greatest Christian mystics, John of the Cross: 'At eventide, (that is at the end of your life) they will examine you on love.' For, as will be discussed more fully in a later chapter, most often God does not meet men directly, he meets them in their neighbour; and the sincerity of men's Christian belief can only be judged by their attitude to him.

For God himself is intensely involved with men, as Christ teaches in various parables on lost things, which he told in response to the complaint of the Pharisees that he received sinners and even had meals with them. If one of you had a hundred sheep, he tells them, and lost one of them—would you not leave the ninety-nine to go and look for the one that had got lost? And, addressing himself to the women: if one of you, he asks, had lost a drachma— the equivalent of a day's wages, say about three pounds of our money—out of her housekeeping money, would you not turn the house upside down to find it and be overjoyed when you had at last done so? But if even these stories should not convince them he tells them another, in much greater detail, about a father whose younger son asks to be given his share of the inheritance, then leaves home and squanders all the money in bad company until he is reduced to a life of abject poverty. Then he realizes his folly and decides to return home, hoping that he will at least be given a menial job by his father and be sure of a roof and food.

But when he arrives in a very contrite frame of mind he has a staggering surprise: his father is so delighted that he has learned his lesson and returned home that he gives him fine clothes instead of his rags and makes a great feast for him, 'because this son of mine was dead and has come to life again'.

This, Jesus teaches the crowds, is exactly how God behaves towards the repentant sinner: however much you may have grieved him, if you turn back and ask to be once more accepted by him, he will receive you with joy and all your misdeeds will be forgiven. For the God that Jesus came to reveal is indeed the completely transcendent God whom no man can see or comprehend, but he is also a God who loves the human beings who are his creatures and wants them to come to him trustingly. He is not, as Aristotle thought, the 'unmoved Mover' of the universe, who himself remains completely aloof from the world he has set in motion; he cares for men as a father cares for his children. For this reason he wants them to pray to him.

It is sometimes asked why prayer should be necessary, seeing that God knows men's needs in any case. Indeed Jesus himself discourages his followers from making endless petitions, for 'your Father knows what things you need before you ask him'. Nevertheless he teaches them to pray, because prayer is something very different from informing God in detail and with much repetition about all one's requirements. We pray, not in order to inform God about things he does not know, but in order to get in touch with him, to acknowledge our dependence on him, to give him the glory that is his due from his reasonable creatures. This is the reason for man's prayer.

It has been said by certain modern theologians that prayer is not an activity apart from other activities, it is not a turning into 'the hidden garden'. Yet Jesus himself told his followers to turn away into their 'inner chamber' and 'close the door' in order to pray, and he himself set apart some hours in the night or withdrew from the crowds to a mountain precisely in order to be away from all distractions and alone with God. If even to him prayer was a separate activity—though, of course, in another sense all his life was prayer—how much more must it not be that for Christians?

God is not the same as the world around us, and if we would bring God to it we must first be in touch with him ourselves. Indeed, if we want to keep the first commandment of loving God above all else with our whole heart and strength, we simply have to pray, prayer being, as the early Fathers explained, communion with God or the lifting of our hearts to him. It would be a strange way of loving our family or friends if we would never set apart some time to be together with them. Certainly, our love for them will be there all the time, even in our professional and other activities; but it would never be there if we did not also meet them personally quite frequently.

Now it must be admitted that only too often Christians have divorced their prayer from their daily life, so that 'saying one's prayers' (a rather unfortunate expression) has become an activity that has lost all connection with one's other activities. It is rather like repeating some set piece which has nothing to do with what we have just done or are going to do and has no influence on our personality at all.

We may also imagine that, while praying, we are turning to someone else outside our world—only to plunge into this latter again when the set time is up. Such a view of prayer, however common it may be, is totally insufficient and is certainly not what Christ or the apostles meant by it. But in that case, what is prayer?

One of the difficulties is that so many spiritual books hardly ever speak about men or persons but about 'souls'. This suggests only too easily that prayer is not an activity of the whole person but only of the 'soul'. Now, as we do not speak about 'souls' in connection with our work or our recreation this unfortunate habit of writers of devotional books makes it appear as if prayer were something quite unconnected with our daily life, from which we have to turn away in order to give ourselves up to converse with God.

But prayer is not an activity of the soul only; it is, indeed, more an action of the whole person than any other. True, when we pray we 'turn' consciously towards God—but this God is not someone at a distance from ourselves. In fact, many of the Christian mystics and theologians have affirmed that God is nearer to us than we are to ourselves. For because he is utterly transcendent, not confined within the limits of time and space, he is always 'present', hence it is always possible for us to 'turn' to him. And we turn to him with our whole human personality, not just with a special part of us which is called the soul and which, as it were, comes into action only when we pray.

This turning towards God is perhaps even better called an 'opening' to him, an opening that will 'let him in'. Again this is, of course, image language, but the relationship between the transcendent God who is yet nearer to us than we are to ourselves can only be expressed in such metaphorical terms. For the whole purpose of prayer is that we should be open to the divine influence and thus be able to be changed into a greater likeness of Christ. Without such an 'opening' of our whole personality in prayer it is impossible to find God, just because we can no longer find him in nature which, as we have seen, has become 'dedivinized' through our better understanding of it.

Now this opening must affect our whole life and all our activities. We need not 'pray about' any of them, but we must lay ourselves open to the goodness, the 'grace', to use a theological expression, that flows out from God. Not that we shall feel it (even though it may sometimes happen that we do). But as God is goodness itself it is impossible that such an openness to God should not have profound effects on our whole personality.

Certainly, men can pray without being 'open', and this is the source of a good deal of criticism and disappointment. 'This person is in church so much and seems always to be saying prayers—how is it possible that he (or, more often she) should be so full of spite and so uncharitable.' The parable of the Pharisee and the publican, to be discussed a little further on, shows quite clearly that there is a kind of prayer that does not open but rather closes a person to the divine influence. God alone can judge the quality of a man's prayer: neither its length nor its frequency has anything to do with it. But a genuine desire to be open to God, to let him really enter into our personality and our life, is itself prayer, as well as being the precondition for it. Prayer related to life, then, is an openness to God; and it is essential if our daily life is to be lived according to his will. Therefore Jesus taught his disciples the Our Father, and Christians have at all times used this and other forms of prayer to approach God.

In the seven petitions of the Our Father man's relation-

ship to God is summed up, and these may again be reduced to the central one: 'Thy kingdom come'. For in the
coming of God's kingdom all desires and prayers of men
and all the commandments of God will be fulfilled. Therefore it is not surprising that this kingdom should be the
subject of a comparatively large number of parables
designed to bring out the various aspects of this mysterious
entity.

These kingdom parables, as they are called, are col-
lected in chapter thirteen of Matthew's gospel. There is
first of all the parable of the sower, whose seeds fell on
four different kinds of ground; by the wayside, where the
birds picked them up, on stony ground, where they could
not develop properly because there was no depth, upon
thorns which choked the young plants, and finally on
good ground, where the seed could grow and yield much
fruit. Here the kingdom is evidently, as the detailed
explanation that follows the parable tells the reader, the
gospel that is preached to all kinds of people and whose
fate depends on the character of those who hear it. The
gospel itself is always good and has all the possibilities
of producing good in those to whom it is preached, but
it does not work by magic: it needs an adequate human
response to become fruitful and, as the parable implies,
in the greater number of cases it does not bring forth the
good results it should, because men place too many
obstacles in its way.

In a second parable the kingdom is again compared
with seed; only this time the seed is all sown in a field.

But while the man who sowed it was asleep his enemy sowed weeds among it. It would not be advisable to remove the weeds at once for fear of rooting up also the good seed; so both have to grow till the harvest, when the two will be separated—the weeds to be burned and the wheat to be placed in the barn. Here the 'kingdom' is obviously no longer the word that is preached but Christendom itself, where the good and the bad flourish side by side, and the parable answers those who are scandalized by this fact.

In the next parable Jesus compares the kingdom to a tiny grain of mustard seed which grows into a very large tree in which many birds find shelter—foretelling the spread of Christianity from very small beginnings into a world religion for all races.

Finally, the kingdom is compared to leaven (or yeast) which a woman folds into the flour until it is all penetrated by it—giving a slightly different slant to the teaching of the previous parable, namely the penetration of the world by the gospel.

But the kingdom which Christ preached has many other aspects, and some of them seem to be mutually contradictory. For, on the one hand, Jesus tells his followers that the kingdom is already there, since he casts out devils by the Spirit of God; it suffers violence, it is among (or within) men, it may be entered by giving up one's riches. On the other hand, however, it is definitely in the future, it is 'eschatological', as in the parable of the king who saw a man without a wedding garment at his feast and 'cast him out into the outer darkness', or in the saying of Jesus

81

at the Last Supper that he will not eat the Passover again until it is fulfilled in the kingdom of God.

If we analyse this teaching on the kingdom still further we shall see that it corresponds to the threefold vocation and destiny of man: it is, first, moral and psychological: the teaching of the gospel accepted or rejected by the individual; secondly, it is a social entity growing from small beginnings to a world-wide phenomenon, whether this be called Christendom or the Church; and, thirdly, it is the ultimate end of man, life after death.

But these three 'kingdoms' are really one and the same and dependent on each other: the individual who has accepted the gospel in full becomes by this very fact a member of the Church and has as such received the promise to reach his final destiny in life after death.

For in the teaching of Christ man is presented in the completeness of his being: as an individual as well as a member of a community. This dual vocation of man, who has to work out his personal destiny within society is already implicit in the dual commandment of love in which Christ himself sums up every law: love of God and love of one's neighbour. But this love has many expressions; indeed, men are so different that it will express itself in as many forms as there are persons. Jesus told the rich young man to give up all his possessions and follow him; he did not, however, ask the centurion to abandon his post and his family. He demanded from some of his disciples that they should lead a single life, be spiritual 'eunuchs' for the sake of the kingdom of heaven; but he

graced weddings with his presence and never so much as
hinted that marriage was an inferior state of life. For
Peter himself was married. And, as we have seen, Christ
liked to use bridal imagery to describe the kingdom of
heaven and his own relationship to men.

In this connection it should also be pointed out that he
himself took a much more lenient view of what is generally
called the 'sins of the flesh' than many later Christian
authorities. Only too often in the history of the Church
has sin almost been equated with sexual misbehaviour. In
this, practice has differed considerably from theory; for
pride, not sexual offences, is the first in the catalogue of
the seven so-called 'capital' sins theologians have drawn
up, and is the root of all others. But this official teaching
has been very largely disregarded, and sins against the
seventh (or sixth, according to another enumeration)
commandment have generally been taken far more seriously than any other.

Now there is no doubt that Jesus considered adultery
and extra-marital relationships as sinful; for he told the
woman taken in adultery (John 8 : 3) to go and sin no
more and the public sinner who washed his feet with her
tears (Luke 7 : 37ff) that her sins were forgiven.

According to the Jewish Law a woman's adultery was
to be punished by death, and a prostitute was despised as
much then as now and was not admitted to any respectable
home. But these two stories show clearly that Jesus considered that both repentance and the forgiveness that
follows it are easier in the case of these sins because they

are not essentially opposed to love. A woman who is carried away by passion or circumstances to commit such sins can often turn to God much more easily than a man who is completely wrapped up in his material possessions or who is so proud of his own achievements that he has no room for any other love.

This, however, does not mean, as certain modern theologians hold, that extra-marital relationships can ever be 'right'. 'What is wrong in ninety-nine cases may be right in the hundredth case', they inform us. But this sounds almost like saying that though twice two make four in ninety-nine cases they may make five in the hundredth. There are absolute norms of right and wrong; neither adultery nor murder can be wrong in some cases and right in others. If this were not so, we should soon go back to the jungle—for who is to decide in which cases these things are right and in what circumstances they are wrong? A murderer may have had every provocation to kill his grandmother because she was a mean and nasty woman who would not make him a sufficient allowance from her wealth so that he could live a full and pleasant life while he was still young enough to enjoy it. But would this make the murder right? A man or woman may commit adultery because they find other partners more satisfactory than their own, claiming overpowering love as their excuse—but does this make adultery right?

This so-called 'situation' ethic, which makes the morality of a course of action depend not on an objective law but on the 'existential' situation in which the persons concerned find themselves, is often claimed to be the only morality acceptable in our time; indeed, Christ's own teaching is said to correspond to it.

But Jesus never said that the public sinner or the woman taken in adultery had done nothing wrong. He accepted their repentance, not their continuance in sin. He always dismissed repentant sinners with the words 'Go and sin no more'—he did not say: in your particular situation you are justified in committing adultery. Certainly, modern thinkers are at liberty to teach such 'situational' ethics, but they cannot in all sincerity hold that Christ himself taught it. Indeed, it is rather odd that for nineteen hundred years none of the Christian churches and denominations has ever interpreted his moral teaching in this way, which, incidentally, flatly contradicts his principle: 'Let your speech be Yes, yes, No, no.'

It is, of course, a very different matter if a man commits a fault against the universal moral law from ignorance. The Japanese who committed harakiri or the Indian widow who would jump on to the funeral pyre of her husband did what they believed to be right, hence they did not 'sin', since they followed their conscience, which must always be the ultimate guide of man.

But Christ did not speak to the Japanese or the Indians, he spoke to the Jews, who had a code which they believed to be the divine law, summed up in the ten commandments, and who therefore knew that adultery and sexual licence were wrong in themselves. The new and liberating teaching he proclaimed was that it was wrong to punish such sins with stoning and ostracism, even after those who had committed them had mended their ways; that all men are sinners in the eyes of God and none have the right to think themselves above their fellow-men.

Therefore Christ's most stringent censures were reserved for those who keep external ceremonies and are outwardly blameless but are inwardly full of envy and hypocrisy, who make for others laws that are impossible to keep but allow themselves every liberty. For these men are so convinced of their own righteousness that they can see only the faults of others and not the much worse ones in themselves. This is the meaning of the saying about the unperceived beam in one's own eye and the clearly seen splinter in one's neighbour's, as well as of the parable of the Pharisee and the publican.

The Pharisees were the most highly esteemed representatives of Israel's religion because they kept the law, especially that of the religious ceremonies, most meticulously, whereas the publicans or tax-collectors were despised because their office brought them into contact with the 'impure' pagan occupation authorities who farmed out to them the right to collect taxes. Moreover, this work was badly paid, so that the publicans normally resorted to extortionist practices on their ignorant fellow Jews. Hence in New Testament times publican and sinner had become synonyms.

In the parable of the Pharisee and the publican, however, Jesus turns this popular estimation of the two upside down. For the Pharisee utters a most self-satisfied prayer, informing God that he fasts and gives tithes regularly and thanking him that he is not like the rest of men, including the publican who is standing at a respectful distance, striking his breast, and saying no more than 'God, be merciful to me a sinner'. And Jesus staggers his hearers by telling them that the man who truly pleases God is not the self-righteous Pharisee but the humble publican who dared not say anything to God but ask mercy for his sins.

It is one of the paradoxes of Christianity that, while making the strictest moral demands, such as those set out in the Sermon on the Mount, Jesus nevertheless liberated men from the sense of guilt and frustration their weakness only too frequently produces.

Today we hear only too much of neuroses and states of anxiety. On the face of them these do not seem to have much to do with guilt; but when we enquire more deeply there is very frequently a profound insecurity at the bottom of them, produced by the uncertainty of men who still have a conscience, but no light to guide it and no power to soothe it when it rebels. They see around them only evil and suffering and there is nothing either to explain or to give them mastery over these dark sides of our experience. Christians claim to have solved the problem of evil and suffering existentially, even though not logically—for it remains a mystery—and so in the following pages we can do no more than throw some light on it in terms of religious experience.

The Problem of Evil and Suffering

Though Christianity offers the most satisfying solution to the mystery of evil and suffering, it is just Christianity from which modern men will often turn away, on the very grounds that evil and suffering exist in the world. For since Christianity teaches that God is a loving Father, a being of absolute perfection who is not only all-good and all-wise but also all-powerful, they cannot understand why there should be so much that appears to be completely negative in this world.

Hence one hears only too often: if there is a God, why does he allow wars, concentration camps, agonizing diseases? How can he permit innocent little children to be cruelly murdered or to die from starvation or cancer?

Or, on an even more personal level, how often people ask: Why had this suffering to happen to me? Why should just I be called on to bear the loss of the person whom I loved most in the world? Why should I have an accident that deprives me of all that made life worth living for me? How can God permit all this? How can there be a good God ruling a world in which Auschwitz and Hiroshima could happen?

Our generation has not been the first to ask these agonizing questions. Jeremiah had already asked: 'Why does the way of the wicked prosper?' and the main theme of the Book of Job is the suffering of the innocent. Job's friends represent the old Jewish idea that suffering is invariably the punishment of the wicked; but Job is not conscious of having done anything wrong and continues to justify himself, to the disgust of his friends, until God himself answers him 'out of the whirlwind'. And the answer God gives is man's ignorance. 'Where wast thou when I laid the foundations of the earth?' Jahweh asks the sufferer and proceeds to enumerate a series of natural phenomena the causes of which man cannot know. 'Hast thou given the horse his might?' God asks scornfully, 'Does the eagle mount up at thy command?' Man is surrounded by mysteries, how does he dare argue with the Almighty? Then Job humbles himself and tells God that he has spoken about things which he did not understand: 'I had heard of thee by the hearing of the ear; but now mine eye seeth thee, wherefore I abhor myself, and repent in dust and ashes.'

This means that Job had so far known God only by

hearsay; but his sufferings have given him a personal experience of his transcendence; Job's question is not answered in human terms, but his difficulties disappear before the overwhelming 'otherness' and power of God. The only attitude that behoves man before God is repentance in dust and ashes.

The answer of the Book of Job to the problem of suffering is a mystical answer. It is the answer of the transcendence of God which has been discussed in the first chapter of this book. But it does not really satisfy the mind of man, which is for ever seeking reasons and desiring justice. Certain Eastern religions as well as the Stoic philosophers have tried to solve the problem of suffering by denying it, rather like some modern sects such as the Christian Scientists, who seek to heal sickness by denying its real existence. If we believe that the world around us does not really exist, that it is but the 'veil of Maya' as the Hindus call it, then evil and suffering do not exist either, they are just as much an illusion as goodness and joy. But the Western mind, whether Christian or not, cannot accept this teaching which contradicts all experience, and even in the East it has been put into practice only by an elite of ascetics; ordinary people there have also accepted the outer world and experienced personal suffering, though it does not constitute such a problem for them, because they do not believe in a personal God who is all goodness.

In other Eastern religions, for example in Persian Zoroastrianism, the difficulty was solved by assuming two equal principles or gods, one good, one evil, in constant war with each other. This, too, is no real solution; it leaves the final outcome undecided and does not answer the innate human desire for the ultimate victory of the good.

Christianity, on the other hand, takes over the Old Testament connection between suffering and sin but, and this is something new (unless we take into account the very difficult passage in Isaiah 42 on the Suffering Servant), it gives suffering a meaning.

First of all, suffering and death are consequences of the fall of man, that is to say of the calamity that befell the first men, which is described in chapter 3 of the Book of Genesis. The account in this chapter comes from an ancient document and it is couched in mythological imagery: there is a wonderful garden, in which Adam and Eve, the first man and woman, live. In this garden there is a tree, the tree of the knowledge of good and evil, of the fruit of which God has forbidden them to eat. But a bad spirit, in the shape of a serpent, persuades Eve to disobey the divine command, and after both she and her husband have eaten God punishes them by expelling them from the garden, making them mortal and subjecting them and their descendants to all kinds of suffering.

Stripped of its mythological elements this story provides an answer to the disquiet of man faced with suffering and death, which in our time has produced a whole philosophy of pessimism whose chief exponents are Sartre and Heidegger, the fathers of existentialism. The Genesis story frees God from responsibility for man's predicament: all man's ills, his *Angst* (a key term of the existentialists, meaning anxiety), his mortality, his subjection to pain and disease, all these are but the consequences of his own disobedience to God. Without this disobedience he would have lived in paradise 'happily ever after'.

Now it may be objected: but why did God allow man to disobey him, as he must have foreseen the consequences of his disobedience? This question is linked to the problem of human free-will and to the mystery of love. God could, of course, have created a creature that would have obeyed him automatically and thus avoided all suffering, but, I would suggest, all true happiness as well. Endowed as we are with free-will, it is as difficult for us to imagine what it would be like to be without it as it is to visualize ourselves existing outside time and space. But probably we would never feel that our actions were our own; we should be impelled by some force to pursue only one course, we would never have the satisfaction of having gained a victory over ourselves. We would have lived lives of automation, as it were, only giving out what was fed into us.

In the nineteenth century, when men were inclined to believe in unlimited progress, it was more difficult to accept such a view of something gone wrong with man and his world than it is today, after two world wars with all their consequences. It has been brought home to us only too poignantly that every invention, every triumph of human ingenuity seems inevitably to bring something evil in its wake: atomic energy, which could—and probably still will—bring untold blessings, is also an instrument of the most ghastly destruction; television is not only a marvellous means of education and entertainment but can also corrupt and sap man's own activity; all the wonderful modern means of transport are also responsible for maiming and killing on a fairly large scale. There simply is no technological advance that does not also inflict suffering and degradation.

Why does the good God, in whom Christians believe, allow this?

There can be no clear-cut answer. The story of the Fall is an attempt to explain evil and suffering, but this explanation certainly has its own difficulties. For does it not offend man's sense of justice that the disobedience of one human couple should be visited by such a deluge of suffering, often inflicted on totally innocent creatures like for example tiny children? More, if suffering is only the punishment for the fall of men, why is there so much of it also in the animal world as St Paul wrote in his Letter to the Romans: 'We know that the whole creation groaneth and travaileth in pain together until now'.

It would seem that the modern theory of evolution accounts for these 'defects' in the world much more easily than the old idea that God created each species separately. For nothing that develops is perfect: it only aims at perfection, it can never reach it. And simply everything in our world is in the process of some sort of development, because we all live in time. Suns and stars evolve, even though we cannot realize it because our lives are infinitely short as compared with those of the heavenly bodies. Plants and animals develop, they grow, reach their full maturity and die, just like men. It is a law of nature that growth involves suffering as well as decay; no sentient being is without a certain amount of suffering in this life.

More, it is not only individual growth that is intimately bound up with suffering; practically all creatures inflict suffering on each other. The worm is eaten by the hen, the hen by the fox, the fox is chased by the hounds; indeed, 'nature is red in tooth and claw'.

And man himself inflicts suffering on all creation, which according to the Biblical account has been subjected to him, when he kills animals either for his food or to defend himself against their attacks. Indeed, suffering in one form or another is bound up with survival, and this form of suffering seems not to be linked directly to moral evil.

But there is another form, which is so linked, and this constitutes the greatest problem. It is the suffering consciously inflicted by men on one another. This means that there is an inclination in men that tends to evil. It exists in all men, but in varying degrees. Today many doctors as well as many legal experts are inclined to attribute all evil, all crime to some psychological maladjustment, and in one way they are more in line with Christian theology than they know. For what theologians call original sin is precisely such a maladjustment, such a lack of balance and harmony that produces neuroses as well as crime.

A passage from St Paul is illuminating on this point. 'To will is present in me' he writes to the Romans (7 : 18f), 'but to do that which is good is not. For the good which I would I do not; but the evil which I would not, that I practise.' This is the confession of human weakness which all of us know in some measure or other. It is not, however, a denial of free will. The will is there, but it is only too often frustrated by the lower instincts of human nature.

This weakness, however, does not remove human responsibility. The man who allows his lower instincts to overpower him is not for this reason guiltless. This he could only be if he were no longer capable of distinguishing right from wrong. Here the theologian parts company with the psychiatrist, who would leave a man no choice. Not only Christianity but our whole moral and legal system is based on the conviction that—apart from certain cases of mental disorder—man is responsible for his actions, that he can avoid evil, and St Paul's words which have just been quoted are no counter-argument. For the point the apostle is concerned to make here is to acknowledge human weakness in general, but only in order to affirm all the more strongly immediately afterwards that this 'law of sin and of death' loses its force in Christ.

The 'law of sin and of death' is the state of man—theologically expressed—'after the Fall', or, in non-theological language, as we find him in the context of the evolutionary process. As nothing is perfect at its very beginning but only tends to perfection in the course of development, so mankind, which according to Teilhard de Chardin will be fulfilled only in the final perfection of 'Omega', must traverse a long history until it reaches the goal of perfect humanity as willed and forseen by God.

Nevertheless, there is evil in the world other than the mere defects of evolution or the weakness of the will described by St Paul. Though philosophers have often defined evil as the absence of good we know only too well from experience that there can be a real 'presence' of evil that hits us in the face. In the cold-blooded murderer there is not only an absence of love, there is a presence of hatred; in the torturers of the Nazi concentration camps there was a cruelty that was far more than the mere absence of gentleness. It is something that cannot be accounted for only by the weakness of the will, it seems something spiritual that enters the very being of a man and takes possession of him.

The Christian explanation of this evil is that it is caused by a fallen spirit, Satan, the angel who rebelled against God, became the devil and now tries to work against God as much as he is allowed and able to do so. In our contemporary Western world it is difficult to believe in spirits, because science and technology, by which our world is so largely ruled, are by their very nature concerned only with matter that can be investigated by the senses and the scientific instruments that are, as it were, their continuation. The world of the spirit and of spirits, on the other hand, is not accessible to scientific investigation; but this does not mean that it cannot exist. Not even the most sensitive instruments can measure love, generosity and the like, yet we all know that they exist in men. Why, then, should it not be possible that spirits also exist, both good and evil ones?

We no longer believe, as did our ancestors, that the material world is governed by or at least subject to the influence of spirits. But if we believe in a God who is Spirit there is no reason why, beside the material creation subject to evolution, there should not also be a spiritual creation, and why this creation should not have some influence on men.

Whether we call the evil spirit the devil or simply the principle of evil, such a principle does seem to be active in the world over and above the defects that are a necessary accompaniment of evolution. The question Christians cannot help asking is why God allows its activity. The traditional answer is that God created all rational beings free so that they might love him not under compulsion but by their own free choice. When some of these beings abused their freedom and turned against God he did not annihilate them but kept them in existence, letting them use their freedom in the way they wished, though subject to his overruling omnipotence. It is this divine respect for the freedom of God's creatures that is responsible for the presence of evil in the world of the spirit, but even from this evil good can come.

In the course of mankind's journey towards the collective perfection of 'Omega' many will approach an individual perfection, even though the goal of mankind in general is still far away. And because universal perfection is not yet, individual perfection will not be reached without suffering, whether it be due to the necessary effects of evolution or be inflicted by one's fellow-men. Now this is the new attitude to suffering, taught by Christianity. Christ himself, both God and perfect man, could fulfil his mission to humanity at that moment of history only by suffering. When he will return in his glory at the end of time, at the point of 'Omega', as Teilhard would say, there will be no more suffering for, in the language of the Bible, he will usher in the new heaven and the new earth, when evolution will have reached its goal and the spirit of evil will have finally been vanquished.

But before mankind can reach this ultimate state evil and the suffering it brings are inevitable; indeed, according to biblical teaching they are integrated into God's plan of salvation. For, paradoxical as it may sound, good can spring from evil, and the greatest good, salvation of all mankind, from the greatest evil, the putting to death of the God-man.

Now even though we may admit that the death of Christ, followed by the resurrection and the spread of Christianity was actually the greatest blessing, can such a principle also be applied to other suffering? What blessing can there be in the murder of a child, in the painful death of a young mother, in the slaughter of millions in war? On the face of it, none. Yet, when we consider the matter more carefully, even the death of a child or a young mother, even the horrors of war may have as their bye-product, so to speak, some purification. The loving acceptance of such catastrophes, the heroic neighbourly love which war often produces alongside all the cruelties, are signs that evil does not invariably bring forth evil but that there is some way of compensating for it, even though the positive seems infinitesimal if compared with the negative results.

Further, in the world as it exists today it seems that without suffering it is virtually impossible for men to develop into integrated and strong characters. Supposing a child were never to encounter opposition, were never ill, were to get all he wanted and were generally only cosseted and admired, the result would be that he would never grow up and would be quite unable to face life; he would never become an adult. True, parental cruelty and lack of understanding may in very many cases have disastrous effects on children; but without any discipline and opposition, which mean a certain amount of suffering for the children, there cannot be a normal development. There is a great deal of truth in the saying from the Book of Proverbs (13 : 24): 'He who spares the rod hates his son; but he who loves him corrects him in time', even though this opinion is very unfashionable at the moment. But it remains to be seen whether the spoilt teenagers of today will not revert to it when they themselves become fathers and mothers; the views some of them already express on the matter seem to point in this direction. Again, all these considerations are not proofs; they are only meant as indications that evil and suffering may have a meaning, even though our limited human intelligence can only get occasional glimpses of it.

But, taking the other view, so often expressed in contemporary philosophy and literature, that it has no meaning, does this not destroy all meaning, not only of suffering and of evil but of life itself? Of course, this is what existentialist philosphers tell us: human life is meaningless.

It is impossible to argue with such a view, as the meaning or otherwise of life is a personal conviction rather than a thesis that can be proved by argument. One might only ask rather maliciously what, if life is meaningless, is the use of writing books about it? Since they, too, must be meaningless.

But we have already seen that the suffering of Christ— and conversely the evil that produced it—must have had a meaning, else there would be no Christianity today. We have also seen that a certain amount of suffering is necessary for the development of the human character in the world as it exists today. We can, moreover, point to an almost unending succession of Christians whose goodness and holiness have developed precisely through great suffering, whether we think of the mental agonies of a St Augustine, the spiritual purifications of the mystics, the physical hardships of the martyrs or the daily sufferings of all true Christians intent on following their Saviour. Suffering, therefore, is not meaningless; it can be turned into maturity, into sanctity even.

It can be so turned—but it need not be. For man has free will, and just as this free will can turn to evil and bring about not only small irritations but terrifying catastrophes, so suffering can also produce bitterness and the warping of character as well as its strengthening and softening.

For there is in nature as well as in human history the possibility of waste. We need only remember the enormous number of seeds that are wasted, both in plants and in animals, including human beings, to realize that waste seems to be a law in the realm of nature as well as in the realm of the spirit. Why this is so we shall probably never know here on earth, but there it is. The bodies of men and women are fitted with cells capable of producing millions of other human beings, yet only a ridiculously small number of them are ever actually born.

Thus also the world is full of suffering capable of perfecting the whole human race, yet only comparatively very few men and women use these sufferings in the way they are meant to be used. But even the lives of these comparative few should suffice to show that evil and suffering, though negative in themselves, can, through the right use of human free will, produce very positive results.

There is, however, yet another solution of the problem of sin and suffering that Christianity offers the believer, and which is at the very heart of its faith: it is belief in eternal life.

The Problem of Life after Death

THAT there is a life after death has been the belief
of many religious faiths, and it has taken various forms.
In such Eastern religions as Hinduism and Buddhism this
life is conceived in a rather impersonal way as union with
the All, the perfect peace of Nirvana where all individuality disappears. The Greeks believed in the shadowy
world of Hades which meant survival, but in a very
attenuated form. The old Germans believed in the Wal-
halla, the realm where the heroes would continue to fight
and feast in more or less the same, if a somewhat glorified,
way as they had done on earth. The Mohammedans
believe in a heaven specially designed for men who will
find there all the pleasures which seemed most desirable
on earth. Among the ancient philosophers Plato was convinced not only of the survival of the soul after death but

also of its pre-existence. He reasoned that, since the soul is rational, it must be akin to the eternal principles of reason, hence be itself eternal. In modern times Emmanuel Kant sought to prove the immortality of the soul on moral grounds. He argued that, because the moral law is eternal and the present life on earth is evidently full of injustice, there must be a future existence in which all justice will be restored.

Indeed, a desire for survival is deeply ingrained in men; it is the obverse of his fear of death. For this fear visualizes something more than only the pains that are most often, though not always, associated with dying. It is concerned principally with the fear of non-existence. There is deep down in man an instinct that is horrified at the mere thought that this particular I that is living at this moment should cease to exist. If we face this instinct sincerely we shall find that we simply cannot imagine how the world is going to continue without us. That there should be a time when we shall no longer be there, when we shall simply have ceased to exist, is a terrifying thought to most of us.

It is this thought that has produced the deeply pessimistic philosophy of existentialism, based on the idea that we come from the nothing and once more go to the nothing, that we are surrounded by nothingness, a tiny flicker of consciousness in the surrounding darkness of non-existence. It is truly a dreadful thought, hence it is not surprising that the existentialist philosophy should be full of dread and *Angst*, because all men's instincts revolt against such an idea. But in the existentialist view of the world these instincts are simply wishful thinking; just because our whole nature seems to revolt against this void that surrounds us we must be heroic and accept it and live with it in spite of *Angst* and dread.

But is this argument really quite sound? There are certain basic instincts in men, the instinct for food, needed for the survival of the individual, the instinct of sex, needed for the survival of the race—and the instinct of survival after death. Nature provides for the satisfaction of the first two instincts; is it not at least reasonable to assume that provision should also be made for the satisfaction of the third?

True, this instinct is not present in all men, there are exceptions—but then, it is the same with the sex instinct, which is also almost absent in some men and women. Nevertheless, the instinct for survival after death is so widespread that it may be called practically universal. Is it so very unreasonable to believe that this instinct, too, will be satisfied in one way or another?

Strangely enough, the ancient Israelites had no idea of life after death. When a man died he was said to go to 'Sheol', but this name of the underworld signified hardly more than the grave; it did not imply survival. For their religion was a corporate religion rather than a religion of the individual; Israel survived as a nation, the father survived in his descendants, the wicked were punished and the good rewarded only in this life—the fallacy of this belief being, as we have seen, the subject of the Book of Job. And because the fact of innocent suffering offended the Jewish sense of justice there developed towards the end of the Old Testament period the belief in a future retribution. This belief, however, did not make as much headway as it might have done, owing to the opposition of the Sadducees, an influential priestly party opposed to all developments in the Jewish religion.

The first mention of a resurrection and future retribution occurs in the last chapter of the Book of Daniel: 'Many of them that sleep in the dust of the earth shall awake, some to everlasting life, and some to shame and everlasting contempt.' It developed further in the time of the Maccabees (in the second century before Christ), who were martyred for their active opposition to the Syrians, in defending their faith against the demands of the pagan oppressors. When one of the famous seven brothers was cruelly tortured and at the point of death he confessed his faith that 'the King of the world shall raise us up who have died for his laws, unto an eternal renewal of life' (2 Maccabees 7 : 9); that this meant a bodily resurrection is clear from the following verses, where the martyr expresses his belief that his tongue and hands which have been cut off will be restored to him in the next life.

The author of the Book of Wisdom, too, believed to have written in the first half of the second century B.C., expresses faith in the after-life and its just retribution, when the 'righteous shall judge nations, and have dominion over peoples' (3 : 8).

In the time of Christ the Pharisees were the most influential representatives of this belief, which was shared by most pious Jews except the Sadducees. Through the resurrection of Jesus this faith received a tremendous impetus; for the risen Christ became the undeniable evidence for the possibility of the bodily resurrection, which he himself had promised his disciples when he told them that those who had done good on earth would come forth to the resurrection of life and those who had done evil would rise again for judgement (John 5 : 29).

This resurrection, however, will not take place until the end of time. What happens in the meantime to the soul, believed to be immortal by itself? One view, shared for example by the fourth century Father, St Ambrose, is that it survives in a state of sleep or partial bliss until it is reunited to its body. But according to the more general opinion, based especially on Christ's own parable of Dives and Lazarus (Luke 16 : 19) and his words from the Cross to the penitent thief (Luke 23 : 43), the soul is judged immediately after death and admitted either to the happiness of heaven or condemned to the torments of hell; according to Roman Catholic doctrine there is also the third alternative of purgatory, a state of temporary punishment in which the soul is purged from its sins and prepared for heaven.

Now this whole Christian teaching on man's life after death presents considerable difficulties to modern man, not the least of them being due to the imagery in which it has often been represented both by poets and painters as well as by preachers. It is a well-known fact that especially the idea of heaven quite often appears repellent to intelligent men and women. They conceive of it as a place

106

peopled by rather smug and 'disgustingly virtuous' indi-viduals where everybody continually sings psalms, waves palm leaves and generally indulges in very boring occupa-tions—and that 'for all eternity', century after century after century.

This is indeed a conception that should terrify even the most courageous of men. It is matched only by the repre-sentation of hell as a fiery pit where devils with red-hot tongs pinch the unfortunate inmates—again for hundreds and thousands of years without end.

Now it is quite true that there is a certain amount of evidence for these ideas in the Bible. In the parable of the rich man and Lazarus Jesus presents the former as tortured by thirst in the flames of Hades, and the Book of Revela-tion pictures heaven as a place of perpetual liturgical wor-ship. Moreover, it is often assumed that, according to Christian teaching, only all the boring people go to heaven whereas the more interesting ones go to hell, and it is certainly true that even a very great poet like Dante did not succeed in making heaven more interesting than hell but rather the reverse.

This somewhat alarming fact, however, is due only to the poverty of the human imagination which cannot con-ceive the reality of divine bliss. Indeed, even in quite ordinary contexts it is much easier to make unhappiness interesting than happiness; an unhappy marriage will normally make a much better novel than a happy one.

These descriptions of heaven and hell, whether Biblical or otherwise, should never be taken literally. As life after death is quite outside our experience and takes place beyond time and space as we know it, it can be expressed in human language only by images and concepts taken from our own world. It must therefore be not only totally inadequate but actually misleading, unless it is realized that all this imagery is only meant to express something that is actually inexpressible.

The very term 'eternity' is impossible to conceive for us timebound human beings. For we imagine it necessarily as an unending succession of time—of millions of years—whereas it is precisely not that. For eternity is opposed to time, is outside time, has no beginning or end as we understand it, hence to think of it in terms of time is to misunderstand it altogether. Eternity has sometimes been called 'the eternal now', a paradoxical expression, but one which conveys its meaning better than the idea of unending time.

It is a state of existence that we cannot conceive, but which corresponds to the human instinct for survival. According to Christian teaching we do not lose our personality in this eternal life, on the contrary, our personality will find in it its ultimate fulfilment, because it will be centred in perfection itself, that is to say in God. In this life on earth so many of our gifts have to be suppressed, because we simply cannot develop all of them in the restrictive circumstances of a brief material existence. But in the eternal now the 'vision of God' will bring all our potentialities to fruition, just as the sun ripens the fruit. For the 'image of God' in man, of which we spoke in the second chapter, is only hidden while he lives on earth, but will appear in all its glory when it is in the presence of its original.

For it is quite true what some modern theologians have pointed out, that our religion has often become too one-sided: that we think of it as a separate activity scarcely connected with our daily life. Therefore we tend also to imagine eternal life as a one-sidedly 'religious' state, an unending worship of God by hymns and prayers. One reason for this idea is the over-emphasis on the division between clergy and laity in some Christian churches. This has led to the very wide-spread view that only 'spiritual' activities such as prayer and public worship are religious and pleasing to God, that everything else is 'worldly' and has no place in 'heaven'. But religion is not a separate activity, reserved for Sunday; the Sunday worship must penetrate into the depth of man's being and affect all his work. The layman's daily labour is just as much service of God as the clergyman's ministry of word and sacrament; there is no reason to believe that there will not be some activity corresponding to it in what is called eternal life.

True, we cannot visualize what form this activity will take; but it does seem reasonable to assume that it will be something entirely satisfying to the whole person, and will depend on this person's particular qualities. The image of a God sitting on a throne letting himself be worshipped expresses only one aspect of the divinity, leaving out of account his creative activity, the tremendous mind that has brought into being our mysterious universe and that is present to ourselves and the world, even if it is not 'in' the world. If we stop to think for a moment how much there is for us to investigate in this small world of ours— is it not at least reasonable to assume that there will be infinitely more for us to see and investigate in the divine mind that has called it into being?

It is the corollary of the divine transcendence discussed in chapter two that even in eternity God can never fully be known by any other being, that there will always be far more of him that is unknown than is known. This should be easier to understand for us than for previous generations, because we realize that even of the material universe man can investigate only an infinitesimal part; the astronomer finds ever new stars, ever new constellations—there is no end to his discoveries. And, as it is with the tremendous universe outside our small solar system, so it seems to be with its tiniest particles: a whole world has been discovered even in the invisible atom which gives up its secrets only under the most powerful microscope.

Should not God, through whom this world has come into being, be able to satisfy all the yearnings for knowledge of the scientist?

But this scientific universe also reflects incredible beauty, therefore God must also be beauty itself in all its aspects, whether we think of the beauty of poetry, of painting, of music, and his vision will satisfy all man's desire for this, not, as it seems to us, only passively by looking on the divine beauty, but also by activating all our own creative capacities for beauty in a way far more satisfying than even the experience of the greatest artist on earth.

This complete satisfaction of all human powers, which are yet never surfeited but are always capable of yet further satisfaction, is what is really meant by 'life eternal'. It is *life* eternal, not stagnation; man, whose faculties are so often thwarted in their development by the circumstances of his earthly existence will, in 'heaven', find perfect fulfilment of all his gifts.

This is what our instinct for justice demands, that all our capacities should one day be used to the utmost, that all that was dwarfed should be developed, all that was developed only to a certain point should attain its full growth. It is this ultimate fulfilment that St Paul has in mind when he writes in his first letter to the Corinthians of the things which our eyes have not seen, our ears have not heard, which even have not entered our heart (that is to say our understanding or imagination), but which 'God has prepared for those who love him'.

Now man is not only soul; he is a compound of soul and body, or, in other words, of an invisible, spiritual and intellectual, and a visible, material part. Throughout our earthly life these two interact constantly; a severe bodily illness can affect the intellect so powerfully that it ceases to work; on the other hand, a man can train and develop his spiritual powers so much that they govern his body. The Indian Yogi offers proof of this and, on a different plane, many Christian martyrs, who sang joyfully even under torture. Nor is this power over one's body restricted to a religious context. In all walks of life men and women have endured intense physical sufferings for the sake of their ideals or of those they loved, without breaking down, and have trained their bodies to perform all sorts of incredible feats. But, whether the state of the body affects the mind or whether the mind governs the body, one is so intimately linked to the other that we cannot imagine a living man without either.

Therefore the Christian religion is not content with the immortality of the soul; it also teaches the resurrection of the body, because the body belongs to man, and even the bliss of the soul in heaven is not quite perfect until it has been re-united to its body 'on the last day'.

This is perhaps the most difficult doctrine of all—the resurrection of the dead. For how can a body that has completely disintegrated thousands of years ago be resurrected? And what age would it have? Would the undeveloped body of a two years old child be still that of a child, and the body of a decrepit old man of ninety be aged? These are questions that are often asked, though they are answered in the New Testament itself.

St Paul discusses the matter of the resurrected body in chapter 15 of his First Letter to the Corinthians, because his converts had asked him in what kind of body the dead were to be raised. The apostle first points out the difference between the seed, for example of wheat, and the plant that grows from the seed. It is the same, he says, with the resurrection body. The original body is a kind of seed, which 'is sown in corruption', but the body that is raised up is something quite different, it is a 'spiritual body', that is to say something other than the body that has died. This difference is confirmed by Christ himself, when he says that in the resurrection there is no marriage, that is to say that there will be no more sex.

But how can even such 'spiritual bodies' be formed if there is nothing left of the original bodies? For the naive idea of the graves opening and releasing their dead on the Last Day can no longer be entertained, seeing that of most men not even a speck of dust will be left. This is certainly a mystery; but a solution has been suggested. Just because the soul without its body is incomplete, it must always have in itself the possibility to develop a body, and this possibility will be actualized in the resurrection, when it will 'grow', as it were, a new, spiritual body, corresponding to the earthly body which was, as it were its 'seed', and which had to die, so that the spiritual body might live.

Where will these new men live? The Book of Revelation (21) speaks of 'a new heaven and a new earth' which will replace heaven and earth as we know it. Again, this is image language, which is made quite clear by the description of this new world in terms of gold and all kinds of precious stones. The main point of it is that in this 'new heaven and new earth' God will reign supreme, and all evil and suffering will have disappeared. It is Christian belief that beyond this world in which men suffer and die, in which cruelty and injustice at times seem to be uppermost, there is another 'world', a spiritual world, in which men will live a new life, both of body and soul, free from all the defects of life on earth.

Where this life will be lived we do not know, as it will obviously be outside our space-time. The terms 'new heaven' and 'new earth' are metaphorical expressions; for throughout the New Testament 'new' always means life in the new era ushered in by Christ. Christ has made all things new, so in his good time heaven and earth themselves will be made 'new', they will become the kingdom of heaven in its eschatological sense, from which all evil has been removed.

But what happens to evil and its representatives? What happens to those men and women who have deliberately and consciously rejected Christ and his salvation? This is the most difficult part of Christian teaching, especially in our own time. For in antiquity and during the Middle Ages people took it in their stride. Dante had no qualms at all about relegating everyone of whom he disapproved to the eternal punishment of hell, and the opinion was even widespread that the happiness of the saved in heaven would be increased by the spectacle of the torments of the damned, while St Thomas Aquinas, following St Augustine, held that the number of the damned was greater than those of the saved.

It must be admitted that to the modern mind the idea of hell is repugnant—again particularly for this reason, that we visualize its eternity as unending time. But hell, like heaven, exists outside time and space as we know it, and we simply cannot apply our crude ideas to it. As all theologians agree, the greatest of its sufferings is the absence of God from those condemned to it; but what form this suffering takes and in what way it is linked to the 'eternal now' we do not know. Nevertheless it does seem reasonable to suppose that a man who has deliberately turned away from God throughout his life and even in the face of death should not be granted the vision of him in the future world—for how could such a man be made happy by the vision of him whom he has always hated? For only such men will be condemned to eternal punishment—and God alone knows who they are.

Even the Roman Catholic Church which officially proclaims some of its members to be saints in heaven has never pronounced anyone to be in hell, not even Judas, the traitor. It is nevertheless Christ's own teaching that sinners will go 'into the unquenchable fire' (Mark 9:43 and elsewhere), hence eternal punishment has always been part of Christian doctrine, however reluctant twentieth-century men may be to accept it. But what exactly this punishment is and what is meant by the image of 'unquenchable fire' we simply do not know.

On the other hand, our modern knowledge of the age of the earth and of man and of past civilizations has made it virtually impossible to assume that all men apart from the Old Testament saints and baptized Christians are damned. This would be impossible to harmonize with the infinite love of God; and nowadays the old adage 'no salvation outside the Church' is being interpreted in a very wide sense indeed.

Christ himself was obviously very generous in his views when he told the religious authorities in Jerusalem that the publicans and harlots would enter the kingdom of God before them, that is to say exactly those who were the least 'orthodox' of his people, just as he held up the despised Samaritan as an example of brotherly love. Therefore eternal life cannot be regarded as a kind of reward for right religious belief; the 'kingdom of God' is in itself a mystery, not a club to which a man is invariably admitted by baptism in a certain Christian communion.

This latter view has often been the cause of much suffering and injustice. It has given rise to such practices as enforced baptism or the compulsory 'conversion' of whole peoples as well as to the burning of heretics. Such a view violates man's most precious possession, his conscience, which alone is his final guide on all matters, including his allegiance to a certain religion or none. But if men sincerely believe—as they did in the Middle Ages and as certain Christians still believe—that unless a person is baptized into a certain communion he will undergo eternal punishment, such practices are indeed understandable.

They are understandable, they are not for this reason excusable. For even the most superficial reading of the New Testament makes it clear that the Christian faith must be accepted freely or not at all. Christ did not force the rich young man to follow him, and when, after he had given his followers the very difficult teaching about eating his flesh and drinking his blood, many of them left him, he made no effort to hold them back, but only sadly asked the twelve who had remained: 'Would you also go away?'

The relation between God and man is a relation of love, and love can never be forced. No man can compel another to enter the kingdom of God; he may show the other the way, but the entry must be made by a free act of the will. More, no man can know what the 'kingdom' really is for another. Salvation is in the hands of God, not of man. One sometimes hears a person say: 'This is such a good man—how can he not be a Christian?' But it would be taking a very narrow view of God if we assumed that for this reason God cannot give this man eternal life. Certainly, Christians believe that theirs is the only true religion, and they must follow in the steps of the apostles and endeavour to spread the 'good news' of the gospel; they must preach it by word or by their life, according to their gifts—but force it on men they cannot.

Nor should they worry unduly if one of their loved ones does not hold the same beliefs—Jesus told his apostles that there are 'many mansions' in heaven, and when they asked him how any one could be saved, he answered 'With God all things are possible'.

True, he also said that the way of life is narrow and that few can find it, because a completely integrated Christian life is difficult, indeed. But this is not meant to limit the mercy of God. It is meant to encourage Christians to follow his own example and not to frustrate the divine design which is the salvation of all men. Apart from this, we do not know what anyone's final destiny will be; and we are warned in the strongest terms not to judge others, because judgement belongs to God alone.

If this chapter sounds rather vague and 'agnostic' this is due to its subject matter. The eschatological beliefs of Christianity are the most difficult to make palatable to the modern world, because, on the one hand, they can only be expressed in highly poetic language and, on the other, our whole civilization is geared to this-worldly concerns and therefore not in tune with eschatology.

Yet there is a widespread interest in the unseen world, as is evidenced by the interest in Eastern religions as well as in spiritualism. In the long run even the most sophisticated television set and the fastest jet liner cannot satisfy man's deepest longings—neither can bring back the friends and relatives he has lost, neither can console him for the certainty of his own death. In one way the existentialists are right to lay such stress on the fact of death, which seems to make nonsense of all our joys and endeavours. Christians, too, used to emphasize this certainty of death—which has become almost an unmentionable word in our society. But they have always seen death not as an end but as a beginning, the start of a new, infinitely fuller and happier life than our earthly existence.

This does not mean that Christians despise this life, far from it. For apart from the fact that, according to Christian belief, our eternal destiny depends on the way in which we have lived here on earth, this life here and now has a value in itself.

It must be admitted, however, that Christians have not always clearly realized this value. Many devout men and women throughout the ages have been inclined to despise all secular activities and lead completely 'other-worldly' lives. Now this attitude to life is far more understandable in Hindus and Buddhists, who hold the outside world to be an illusion, than in Christians, who believe in the incarnation and hence in the value of the body and all that pertains to physical life. For it is quite impossible that men should lead an entirely 'spiritual' life on earth: the very need for food, clothing and shelter precludes this.

But because man has not only a body but also a brain, and an inventive brain at that, he has never been content with merely satisfying these needs but has developed all manner of not directly necessary activities from the very beginning: he has sung and painted and composed poems, he has invented tools and later machines of increasingly complicated design, he has thought out philosophical systems and has experimented with nature and so created what Teilhard de Chardin called the 'noosphere', the sphere of the mind. Surely all these activities must have some value in themselves, for they have not only completely changed the world but also developed man himself into a more sensitive and more highly differentiated being than he was in the beginning.

True, as has been shown in the preceding chapter, these activities have also had their bad effects; nevertheless no sensible person could deny that they have created a vast wealth of values of almost incredible diversity. Is it to be believed that these should have no meaning at all for the future life of men, that they should simply be disregarded as if they had never existed?

The great Christian theologians such as St Thomas Aquinas have never assumed that religion could exist in a vacuum. According to the principle that grace builds on nature they have accorded their full importance to all the natural activities of man. The restriction of religion to one narrowly defined sphere of human life has done untold harm to the cause of Christianity, especially since the end of the Middle Ages, when men once more began to discover the independent value of so-called secular activities and when many Christians were frightened that these might do damage to their religion. Hence the condemnation by both Catholics and Protestants of the new astronomy bound up with the names of Copernicus and Galileo and the development of science, philosophy and many other subjects outside the narrowly religious orbit.

But these 'secular' pursuits are as necessary to the development of an authentic 'Christendom' as the strictly religious activities. For all are inescapably integrated into the whole course of evolution; they are all in the final analysis directed towards 'Omega', the ultimate fulfilment of God's design, to which all our work, our inventions, our sufferings contribute in some way. For Christianity is both an other-worldly and a this-worldly religion—it could not be otherwise with a religion which centres in a

God who was made man. And because God was made man, Christianity is in a very special sense the religion of encounter, of the personal encounter between Creator and creature.

The Mystery of the 'Encounter'

MAN does not live alone on this earth. He is surrounded by 'nature', by plants and animals, above all by his fellow human beings. Therefore 'meeting', 'encounter', is his very first experience. The newborn baby already meets the world outside the womb and greets it with a cry. He meets his mother, his father, his nursery, sun and rain, cats and dogs, trees and flowers, and in one way or another they all make an impression on him and he reacts to this impression. He is 'formed' both by the qualities he has inherited and by his surroundings, his encounters with men and their world, and his reactions to these surroundings will gradually help to build his character. These encounters will also, and this is most important, develop his mind. For the child cannot teach himself; he must first learn from others, and he must take their teaching on trust.

If we come to think of it, it is quite extraordinary how much we take on trust. Not only the child, but hundreds of millions of adults have no chance of verifying that the earth travels round the sun, that Italy is shaped like a boot and that Tokyo has ten million inhabitants—let alone all the facts of history which they learn. We simply have to take on trust 1066 and all that—for how many of us can study the relevant documents? All this we take in our stride; but when it comes to the experience of God of which religious men and women tell us we are very much more sceptical.

Now this is not surprising; for whereas the facts of science, literature, history and the rest are within our own orbit even though we cannot verify them individually, the facts of religious experience are very often quite outside our ken. More, they take such very different forms. The Christian mystics claim to be united to Christ, the Quakers believe themselves guided by an inner light, the Hindu loses his individuality in the bliss of becoming all things, the Buddhist believes he enters the ineffable state of Nirvana. But they all have this in common: they testify that there is an experience that raises them above everyday life into a sphere that is no longer part of their ordinary existence. In this experience they are absorbed in, or united to something that is greater, higher than themselves, that enlarges or surpasses their normal consciousness.

The experience of being in touch or in union with the transcendent is quite universally attested. It is only our rather narrow-minded contemporary Western civilization that will not accept even the possibility, let alone the fact, of such experiences. Now it is quite true that many of the phenomena surrounding them can be explained psychologically; further, often so-called 'mystical' experiences are no more than strange psychological states. But the fact that there are spurious 'mystical' experiences does not mean that there cannot for this reason be authentic ones; just as the fact that there exists a paralysis of the limbs that is hysterical does not mean that organic paralysis cannot exist.

Now all these men and women we call mystics are firmly convinced to be at certain times in touch with a power greater than anything in the world our senses can perceive. In all other spheres we believe what the experts tell us, even though we are quite unable to verify it ourselves. Only in the religious sphere are we very unwilling to do this. 'I have not experienced it myself, therefore I won't believe it.' Yet the mystics are, as it were, the experts of the divine, and they are unanimous in their witness to the possibility of encountering it even in this life.

A Christian should be even more ready to believe in the possibility as well as the fact of such an encounter than members of other religions. For in Christ men have actually met God in the flesh, and through him they continue to do so both in the sacraments of the Church and in their personal life. The encounter of Christ in the sacraments will mostly be an encounter in the darkness of faith, though for many Christians this sacramental meeting between man and God has also taken the form of a mystical experience. But whatever the form, this sacramental meeting is a true encounter between creature and Creator, made possible through the incarnation.

However, God is not necessarily encountered only in the religious context of properly mystical and sacramental experiences, which are given only to a comparatively small number of men and women. He has provided us with a far more universal way of meeting him, a way which needs no special, supernatural experience. According to Christ's own teaching he is met in our neighbour: 'As long as you did it to one of the least of my brothers, you did it to me.' In this sense our fellow-men themselves take on the quality of a sacrament; we encounter Christ in them. Seeing Christ in our neighbour sounds like one of these glib and unreal religious statements which are made quite easily but have no proper relevance to our life. Our fellow-men are usually not a bit like our conception of Christ; they are often irritating, unlikeable, annoying, even hostile to us—how can we imagine them to be Christ?

But we are not asked to imagine them to be Christ, we are asked to realize that they share their humanity with Christ as well as with ourselves and to treat them therefore according to the so-called Golden Rule: 'Do to others as you would be done by.' And this means, above all, never to treat our fellow-men only as means towards an end, a view shared by many non-Christian thinkers, for example Kant. No man wants to be treated simply as an instrument for somebody else's use; he wants to be recognized as a person in his own right, with his own aspirations and his own dignity. As soon as he is merely used for the profit of another he will feel degraded; so much social and racial discontent springs precisely from this root, that men have not treated each other as persons, that it has never occurred to them to see Christ in others.

True, in our modern mass society it is very difficult to do this; we cannot consciously see Christ in all the many people with whom we are in daily contact—the bus conductor, the shop assistant, the hotel manager, the waiter in the restaurant and innumerable others. Nor can there be the personal relationship between employer and employee in a modern industrial concern such as existed in a small family business. Christ himself did not mean that when he told his hearers the parable of the Good Samaritan. The Samaritan would normally have taken no notice of the man who 'went down from Jersualem to Jericho' if he had simply met him on his way. But the man had been wounded and robbed, therefore the Samaritan quickly went to his aid. It is particularly the man who needs me who is my neighbour, and who therefore takes the place of Christ in my life. (This, of course, does not mean that social services and other large organizations concerned with relieving the needs and sufferings of men are not based on Christian principles. Here we are only concerned with the *personal* encounter of Christ in our neighbour.) The same teaching emerges from the description of the Last Judgement: Christ appears in the thirsty, in the naked, in the sick—in short, in all those who are in need of help.

In Christian neighbourly love it is not mutual sympathy or common interest that constitute the link between persons but the need of the one and the readiness to help of the other. For this reason Christ can command even the 'love' of one's enemy. Love in the ordinary sense, that is to say liking and affection, cannot be commanded; but love in the sense of helping the other as we ourselves would like to be helped is a very different thing; and such love can be extended even to an enemy. It means, however, the conquest of our natural feelings. We have to realize that in this man in need, whether friend, enemy, or someone unknown, we do meet Christ asking for help. This makes Christian charity different from mere humanitarian assistance. Certainly, social services are necessary and desirable. But they are not enough, and only too often even in such a relationship the man who is helped becomes merely a case, a number; he is not treated as a complete human being and a child of God.

But in the authentic exercise of Christian charity a man is seen as a representative of Christ; his very need, far from being regarded as humiliating, invests him with the dignity of the Sufferer on the Cross, 'As long as you did it to one of the least of my brothers, you did it to me.' A 'brother' of Christ will never become a mere case to be dealt with, and the man who tends him will through him truly encounter God.

There is a charming story about the fourth century saint Martin of Tours who, when still a catechumen and a soldier in the Roman army, divided his cloak and gave half of it to a beggar. In the following night Christ appeared to him in a vision, clothed with half the cloak, saying: 'Martin the catechumen has given me this cloak'. Soon afterwards Martin left the army and was baptized. Here Christ identifies himself with his poor just as, for example, in St Paul's great vision on the way to Damascus he identifies himself with the persecuted, asking the future apostle: 'Why do you persecute me?'

Through the incarnation, therefore, when God assumed man's nature, it has become possible for men to represent God, for men to meet God in their fellows. This is the mystery of the encounter, that God is met in the suffering brother, that in serving the brother we are serving God. It is not necessary to realize this consciously. St Martin was only afterwards given to understand that in clothing the beggar he had clothed Christ; and in the story of the Last Judgement the good ask when they saw Christ hungry or thirsty. The loving attention to the needs of one's neighbour is in itself an encounter with God; hence Master Eckhart, the fourteenth century German Dominican, said that even if he were engaged in the highest contemplation and a beggar asked him for a bowl of soup he would leave his prayer and attend to the need of the beggar.

Indeed, all the Christian mystics are agreed that the exercise of neighbourly love is one of the arguments for the authenticity of the mystic experience; without this love the experience cannot be genuine. Our relation to our neighbour is the touchstone of our relation to God; as St John said: 'If a man say, I love God, and hates his brother, he is a liar; for he who loves not his brother whom he has seen, cannot love God whom he has not seen' (1 John 4: 20). Certainly, just because we have 'seen' our brother it is often very difficult to love him; but to assert that we love God without loving our neighbour is just an empty statement, because God cannot be loved in the void, as it were. Jesus himself said: 'If you love me, you will keep my commandments', and these commandments are summed up in the twofold love of God and our fellow-men. Love must be expressed by deeds; else it is nothing but a mere emotion which does not deserve the name of love.

Thus in this world our fellow-men represent God for us, we meet him in them, and our attitude to him must be judged by our attitude to them. It is one of the great tragedies of Christian history that this has so often been forgotten, especially by representatives of Christianity in high places. When the 'most Christian kings' exploited their subjects to be able to live in absurd luxury themselves, when the church-going upper classes in many European countries treated their 'inferiors' only as means to keep up what they considered their necessary standard of life, when all too many who called themselves Christians turned away like the priest and the Levite from those in need, Christianity lost the masses, because, as Jesus himself expressed it, the salt had lost its savour.

When the Christian no longer encounters Christ in the needy, Christianity must necessarily atrophy. In the first centuries of our era it conquered Europe, because the pagans were profoundly impressed by the mutual love of Christians. When this love is no longer evident it is only to be expected that Christianity should lose ground.

It is very unfortunate that our statistics-conscious time should judge even the health of a Christian community by numbers. So many people made their Easter Communion, so many attended this or that service, so many watched such and such a religious television programme. But what does this mean in terms of the encounter as we have just discussed it? If, say, five thousand members of a parish have made their Easter communion, does this say anything about the vigour of a truly Christian life? Will they for that reason abandon sharp practices in their business, treat their employees as they themselves would be treated, will they have a greater awareness of the presence of Christ in their fellow-men? For these are the things that count; and fifty Christians who are really Christians at heart are better and will have a greater effect on the community than five thousand who only attend services without realizing Christ in their lives.

This is really a commonplace; but it needs to be stressed in our time, because the vigour of the Christian life is only too often equated with numbers. But it is not numbers that count, it is the intensity of the Christian life of the individuals within the community. For if we have so far stressed the encounter of Christ in the needy, there is also another encounter; the encounter of Christ in the true Christian, the saintly man or woman who mirrors Christ in his or her life.

The Mystery of the 'Encounter'

In our time 'saintly' or 'holy' is only too often confused with goodie-goodie. So many of us think immediately of a person who turns in horror from the seamy side of life, who is preoccupied with the immorality of bikinis, thinks sex nasty and grudges young people their enjoyment. But prudery and squeamishness have nothing to do with holiness: quite the contrary, for they are signs of a narrow and often even perverted mind. Christ himself met sinners and, to the horror of the devout and prudish Pharisees, even ate with them. For he had come to call sinners, and not the self-righteous who were sure of knowing all there was to know about God and virtue.

The Christian saint must necessarily imitate his master —hence he, too, will mix with those who come his way, and will seek to help all who need his help. Above all, he will give them his sympathy and understanding, he will never look down on them. And in this understanding, this readiness to help without sermonizing they will meet Christ, as they themselves represent Christ for the Christian who assists them. It is a strange and mysterious interchange, the Christlikeness that helps and the Christlikeness that is helped; but this encounter of Christ with Christ, as it were, takes away all that so often mars the relation between the needy and his helper, that is the feeling of inferiority of the former and the temptation to overbearing behaviour on the part of the latter. In this way the encounter will be fruitful for both, not only materially but also spiritually, because both will have met Christ in the other.

As in the case of the sacraments, this encounter will, of course, take place in the darkness of faith. But from this darkness there may sometimes emerge a ray of light, when Christ becomes a palpable experience at the centre of the encounter. This will then be a true mystical experience, as real as the experience of union in the solitude of mystical prayer. Certainly, these are rare moments, granted to rare people. But they are not essentially different from the dark faith in which these meetings of men in Christ ordinarily take place. The only difference is that what happens in a hidden way is suddenly brought to light.

Today the word encounter, which has been used so frequently in these last pages, has become one might almost say fashionable in another sense: we speak and read constantly of the ecumenical encounter, the meeting of Christians of various churches and denominations with each other. Whereas in former centuries controversy was the order of the day, each party trying to show the other how right it was itself and how wrong its opponents, in the last decades Christians of all communions have been trying to meet not in order to attack, but to understand each other, explaining their own views and listening to those of the others. For we have at last understood that Christ is not only to be met in our own church but also in others; that his Spirit is active in all of them, though in different ways and to a greater or lesser extent.

For today the Christian way of life is attacked from all sides, not only by militant atheism but also by the far more insidious materialism of the 'affluent society', even by a certain section of those professing themselves to be Christians, who, thinking probably in all sincerity to do a service to their religion, want to bring both the religious beliefs and the moral teaching into line with contemporary views.

Now it is, indeed, of the highest importance that Christianity should be presented to our contemporaries in a language they can understand and that its relation to modern science and scholarship should be fully discussed. But what cannot be done, and what will in the last analysis be a service neither to Christianity nor to our society, is to jettison all Christian beliefs as outmoded and to demand a 'non-religious' interpretation of the gospel for the modern world—whatever that may mean. For no genuine Christian has ever held that Christianity is easy, that the demands it makes on men can be fulfilled without a true *metanoia*, a repentance, a re-thinking, a complete renewal of life—or, as St Paul expressed it, a burial of the 'old man'.

Both Jews and Greeks of the early centuries of our era found it as difficult to believe in the resurrection and the divinity of Christ as any contemporary agnostic. When certain of Christ's own disciples found his teaching on the eucharist (John 6) too hard to understand they left him —but he did not water down his doctrine in order to keep them. We simply have to accept the fact that even when Christianity has been presented in modern terms there remains a body of teaching that has to be accepted by anyone who wishes to become a Christian and which is supernatural, that is to say which transcends our natural understanding.

For the ecumenical no more than the mystical encounter can take place on a purely natural plane. When Christians meet to discuss their differences they do not meet like philosophers or historians each giving an account of his personal system or research. They meet as representatives of their various churches to give an account of the tenets of these churches and to compare them with those of other Christian communities, not in order to prove themselves right but to find whether they themselves may not have neglected one aspect of the truth or, conversely, whether they might not have to teach others something that is missing in their presentation of the gospel.

There is even more to these encounters than mere friendly discussion of differences. To be truly Christian encounters they must be animated by love. In the famous thirteenth chapter of his First Letter to the Corinthians St Paul has a good deal to say about love, which is directly applicable to ecumenical encounters, indeed, it might be called a charter of ecumenism. For, he writes, 'Love is long-suffering, is kind . . . is not puffed up, seeks not its own, is not provoked, takes no account of evil, rejoices not in unrighteousness but rejoices in truth, bears all things, believes all things, hopes all things, endures all things; love never fails.'

'Love is kind . . . rejoices in truth'. Only too often in the past Christians have thought it right to throw kindness to the winds in defending what they held to be the truth;

and even today some believers are afraid of sacrificing the truth if they show kindness to those holding a different opinion. On the other hand, quite a number of Christians of all denominations think that in order to be 'ecumenical' they must water down their own beliefs and just be 'friendly' all round. But indifference to religious beliefs is exactly the opposite to true ecumenism. Love, as St Paul says, rejoices in truth, it does not rejoice in error. But it is not provoked by error and takes no account of the evil those in error might do; for it is prepared to endure all things because it also 'hopes all things'.

Endurance and hope are perhaps the most necessary characteristics of those active in the work of ecumenical love. For there is no shortcut to unity; the centuries old differences are far too deep. To heal them we shall probably still have to endure them for a long time, but unless we carry on without ever losing hope, Christian unity will never be established.

Christians believe that the phenomenon of ecumenical encounter has been brought about by the Holy Spirit, the divine Spirit of love himself. But God works through human instruments, and these instruments do not exist in a vacuum, they live in a historical moment shaped by the traditions of past centuries as well as by the aspirations of the present, and the past cannot suddenly be shed at the drop of a hat. It can only be slowly transformed by the contemporary forces working as a leaven in the dough of history.

The ecumenical encounters, animated by the spirit of

Christian love, are such a leaven, which must be allowed to work within Christendom. If they continue, side by side with the personal encounters of the divine of the mystic and the encounters of Christ in our neighbour they will bear the fruit of unity when the time is ripe for it.

Conclusion

In the foregoing pages it has been attempted to present some of the basic tenets of Christian belief in a form which, it is hoped, will be acceptable to the contemporary enquirer. We have not tried to water down such central points as the transcendence of God, the divinity of Christ and eternal life in such a way as to make them meaningless. For we do not think such a procedure would be fair either to Christianity or to this elusive being, 'modern man'. Christianity has always been a 'supernatural' religion; it cannot be anything else if it is to remain Christianity. For it stands and falls with belief in a personal God and in the incarnation of his divine Son, Jesus Christ.

But what has to be done—and we hope to have made our very small contribution in this respect—is to explain it in

terms that can be understood without a knowledge of
theological intricacies and technicalities. For its founder
meant it to be a religion for all men, and his great apostle
Paul of Tarsus became 'all things to all men, that I may
by all means save some' (1 Corinthians 9 : 22).

Yet for all this design of universality, the Christian
religion is a religion—a term which means 'binding';
it has to be accepted on its own terms; we cannot dictate
our terms to it according to our liking. Many of its sayings
are 'hard', they were so even for Christ's contemporaries,
but he never softened them in order to please those who
found them hard.

But two facts have done Christianity untold damage:
the one is that it originated in a civilization quite different
from our own, the other that it is taught to children from
a very early age and that the teaching suited to them is
generally far too little modified when they have reached
greater maturity. The much more concrete language of the
Bible has to be translated into our modern abstract idiom
and the idea behind the image has to be distinguished from
the picturesque form in which it is expressed. This is very
often not done, and so mature men and women still have
images of a superman somewhere above the clouds
directing their lives.

Consequently this direction, too, is visualized as a constant supervision of all our activities. The child has been
told: 'You must not do this, because God sees you';
the man still thinks that Christianity believes in a God who
is, as it were, constantly looking down on him, either

approving or disapproving of whatever he does. It is only to be expected that a grown-up man has no use for such a divine schoolmaster and so very often gives up his religion altogether.

Perhaps what we need today is a greater emphasis on the mystery of the divine Being, a less cut-and-dried presentation of religion. Another name for this mystery is transcendence, which in some theological circles seems to have become almost a dirty word. But unless God is transcendent, that is surpasses not only this visible world but our understanding and our imagination completely, he cannot be God. Why is it that some of our contemporaries are so very reluctant to accept a really transcendent God who is nevertheless in contact with man? Why are they inclined rather to speak about 'the beyond in our midst' and about Christ as the 'man for others'?

Such language, while really explaining nothing, has yet a twofold advantage: on the one hand it leaves both the conception of God and the person of Christ completely in the dark; on the other, neither God nor Christ, seen in this way, have any authority to make demands on men. A religion based on such principles—or should they rather be called anti-principles, analogous to the modern anti-hero—however sincerely held by their representatives, is no religion, because it 'binds' men to nothing, neither to a definite belief nor to a definite ethics.

It starts from the premise that 'modern man' is fundamentally different from all men that have gone before, that he has 'grown up' and no longer needs either a God who is above him (in a non-local sense, of course) nor a moral code. But this implies that he is no longer a sinner, that he is, as Nietzsche expressed it, a 'super-man', 'beyond good and evil'.

One look at the world around us, one glance at the newspapers or at television must surely convince us that this is a wholly unrealistic attitude. The main trouble with the novel interpretation of religion seems to be that those who attempt it see 'modern man' as an ideal being who no longer needs the laws and sanctions of a bygone age. Traditional Christianity's view of man has always been much nearer the facts, and unfortunately these facts, that is to say human nature, have changed very little, despite all our scientific advance, and our more developed social sense—itself, as we have seen, a development of the Christian roots of our civilization. Man is still a sinner, he still needs objective guidance to show him what is right and what is wrong, he still needs, above all, forgiveness. And who can give him that except a God who transcends man's own being, a God who can penetrate his heart because he is in very truth his Creator and his Father?